The NCTE Chalkface Series

D1451490

Studying Literature

student audience

Brian Moon

Studying
Literature

New Approaches to Poetry and Fiction

Originally Australian

National Council of Teachers of English
1111 W. Kenyon Road, Urbana, Illinois 61801-1096

Staff Editor: Thomas C. Tiller

Interior Design: Richard Maul

Cover Design: Pat Mayer

Permissions: Kim Black

NCTE Stock Number: 48719-3050

First published in Australia in 1990 by Chalkface Press, P. O. Box 23, Cottesloe, Western Australia 6011.

It is the policy of NCTE in its journals and other publications to provide a forum for the open discussion of ideas concerning the content and the teaching of English and the language arts. Publicity accorded to any particular point of view does not imply endorsement by the Executive Committee, the Board of Directors, or the membership at large, except in announcements of policy, where such endorsement is clearly specified.

Library of Congress Cataloging-in-Publication Data
Moon, Brian.
    Studying literature: new approaches to poetry and fiction/Brian Moon.
       p. cm. — (The NCTE Chalkface series)
    Includes bibliographical references.
    ISBN 0-8141-4871-9 (paperback)
      1. Readers (Secondary) 2. Literature. I. Title. II. Series.
    PE1121.M68 2000
    808—dc21

                                                    00-027465

Series Foreword

Twenty years ago we judged the success of our students' responses to a reading assignment by the similarity of their responses to a text with ours. We saw it as our job to help students read well, to read with understanding, to read correctly; in other words, we did our best to make students read as we read. We gave little thought to the processes and experiences at work that make a single reading of a text impossible and often even undesirable. We learn much, thank goodness, as we teach. By now we have learned to encourage our students to read diversely, to recognize the processes interplaying and influencing their readings, to examine the cultural factors influencing and the cultural consequences resulting from their reading practices.

Moving beyond encouragement to effective, integrated instruction and practice is always difficult. That is why we are so excited about the NCTE Chalkface Series. Never before have we seen such practical methods of examining and understanding the personal and cultural influences that affect students' reading. The lessons actively engage students and make the invisible processes of reading explicit, demystify responses to literature, and help students understand the myriad factors influencing their reading. These books, like no other secondary reading texts we have come across, had us seeking out colleagues to share our excitement about published lessons. We now do so at every opportunity.

Among the specific strengths in the books are the inclusion of theory and of questions that provide the basis for the applications/student practices. For example, in *Literary Terms: A Practical Glossary*, the study of each term is developed as a mini-lesson, including a short piece to help students with mind-set, a brief theoretical explanation, an activity that requires application, and a summary. Some terms are very common, such as *author* and *character;* others are less common, such as *polysemy* and *poststructuralism*. The material is student-accessible; the format is somewhat different from the traditional glossaries of literary terms. Students and teachers should find the activities very useful illustrations of the terms' definitions and the theories that serve as the foundations of the study of literature.

Gendered Fictions, another title in the series, operates essentially from the premise that texts offer differing "versions of reality" rather than a single illustration of the real world. The authors contend that we are conditioned to make sense of text by reading from a gendered position. They offer many opportunities for students to accept or challenge particular ways of looking at masculinity or femininity. A major question proposed by the text is *how* readers read—a critical question if we want our students to be analytical readers. Perhaps equally basic, the text encourages students to look at how they become what they become. As is true of the other books, the approach is not didactic. Questioning, yes; deterministic, no.

Reading Fictions follows similar assumptions: texts do not have a single, definitive meaning; rather, meaning depends on a number of variables. The authors do suggest that a text may very well have a *dominant* reading (i.e., what a majority of readers may agree is there), but it may also have *alternative* readings (i.e., what other readers may believe is there). The intent is to have students look at various texts and consider what may be a dominant reading or an alternative reading. Again, the intent is to facilitate skill, not to determine what students should believe.

Reading Hamlet positions *Hamlet* as a revenge tragedy and provides students with a context by offering a brief look at other revenge tragedies of roughly the same period: *Thyestes, Gorboduc, The Spanish Tragedy,* and *Titus Andronicus.* That may sound overwhelming; it is, rather, illustrative and offers a genuinely effective context for the study of *Hamlet.* The text also offers a number of ways for students to study character as well as opportunities for student performance. The performance component, in particular, gives students the opportunity to be actively involved with text. The author does not assume that students have to be talented actors.

Studying Poetry again offers opportunities for student performance, considerations of what poetry is, and exercise in writing critiques of poetry. Poems chosen for study range from traditional to contemporary. The book strongly encourages students to identify their own favorite poems, a practice also promoted by America's current poet laureate, Robert Pinsky.

Studying Literature goes to the fundamental question of what makes a piece of writing "literature," asking students to consider features of writing along with their own beliefs and values and encouraging them to reflect critically on the nature of the activity in which they are engaged rather than merely engaging in it.

Reading Stories lays a firm foundation for students moving toward becoming critical readers. From exploring their own expectations prior to reading a work (or rereading one) to questioning authorial intent to exploring cultural and social assumptions, this book makes explicit both the ways in which readings are constructed and the bases on which students might choose among them.

Investigating Texts builds on that foundation by exploring the deeper questions of how texts are made, how ways of reading change, and how texts can be read differently. As in all the books, numerous activities are provided to facilitate such exploration and application, promoting student interaction, an active relationship with the texts provided and, by extension, an active relationship with new texts they encounter.

We are delighted that NCTE has arranged to make Chalkface books available to its members. We are confident that teachers will share our enthusiasm for the publications.

Richard Luckert
Olathe East High School
Olathe, Kansas

William G. McBride
Colorado State University
Fort Collins

Contents

Acknowledgments

Sincere thanks to: Sean Monahan, Dr. David Buchbinder, and Dr. Barbara Milech for much helpful advice; Bronwyn Mellor for her thorough and thoughtful editing; Dr. Annette Patterson for constructive comments on the manuscript; Maurice Jones for suggestions regarding texts; Stephen Mellor and Peter Forrestal at Chalkface Press; Stephen Nichols for perceptive comments; and Annette Moon for constant support and encouragement.

Permissions

Grateful acknowledgment is made for the following permissions to reprint previously published material in this book.

"A Night of Frost and a Morning of Mist" is from *Snowman, Snowman: Fables and Fantasies* by Janet Frame. Copyright © 1962, 1963 by Janet Frame. Reprinted by permission of George Braziller, Inc.

The poem "Beauty" is from the book *The Fat Black Woman's Poems* by Grace Nichols published by Virago Press, London.

Alix Chmelnitzky for "Rest in Peace" in *The Anduril,* edited by F. Courtney and K. Marais de la Motte, St. Hilda's ASG Publications, Mosman Park, Australia, 1998.

Reed Educational and Professional Publishing for "I Know a Man" by Robert Creely in *Mainly Modern,* edited by John Colmer, Rigby Heinemann, Adelaide, 1969.

Penguin Books Australia Ltd. for "Weevilly Porridge" by Eva Johnson in *Inside Black Australia,* edited by Kevin Gilbert, 1988.

Linton Kwesi Johnson for "Yout Scene" in *Dread, Beat 'n Blood* by Linton Kwesi Johnson, Bogle-L'Ouverture Press, London, 1975.

Pam Ayres for "Good-Bye Worn Out Morris 1000" in *All Pam's Poems* by Pam Ayres, Hutchinson, London, 1978.

"Phone Call" by Berton Roueche is reprinted by permission of Harold Ober Associates Incorporated. First published in *The New Yorker.* Copyright © 1965 by Berton Roueche.

HarperCollins*Publishers* for "School" in *The Unploughed Land* by Peter Cowan, Collins/Angus and Robertson, New South Wales, 1958.

Hamlyn Books for the extract from "Leisure" by Ian Moffitt in *This Is Australia,* edited by Rudolph Brasch, published by Paul Hamlyn, Sydney, 1979.

"The Aim Was Song" and "Never Again Would Birds' Song Be the Same" by Robert Frost are reprinted from *The Poetry of Robert Frost,* edited by Edward Connery Lathem. Copyright 1942, 1951 by Robert

Introduction

In recent decades, the study of literature as an academic subject has undergone significant changes. New theories including structuralism, reader-response theory, and deconstruction have challenged traditional approaches to literary criticism. These new methods have expanded the focus from "writers and their works" to encompass the study of readers and their practices, as well as the social contexts in which writers and readers act.

Studying Literature offers high school students an introduction to literary studies that acknowledges these new perspectives. Drawing on contemporary theories and approaches, the book helps students investigate the values, assumptions, and practices that underlie literary activities. It introduces important concepts such as: the social contexts of literary practice; dominant and resistant readings of literature; "gaps and silences" in texts; and issues of race, class, and gender.

The book's opening chapter explores the very concept of literature by testing traditional views and the unstated assumptions that students may bring to literary studies. It shows that the literary qualities once regarded as properties of the text may be in part the product of social practices previously regarded as lying "outside" the text—practices such as reading, teaching, and publishing.

The second chapter applies this new concept by exploring ways of reading literary texts as "cultural artifacts" rather than "personal expressions." It introduces the concept of reading practices: those rules or procedures by which readers make meaning with text. The chapter then goes on to consider where these practices come from and to distinguish between dominant and resistant practices and their effects.

The final chapter examines in detail one aspect of contemporary critical practice: the issue of gender. Focusing on both feminism and masculinities, this section of the book gives students a taste of how the new approaches to literature work in practice, while at the same time pointing out relationships between literary studies and issues of social justice.

With this compact introduction, it is hoped that students and teachers can embark on a more purposeful and rewarding study of literary texts and the institutions that surround them.

1 What Is "Literature"?

- What makes a piece of writing "literature"?
- Who decides what is literary and what isn't?
- What can be learned from studying literature?
- Is literary study about particular kinds of books or particular kinds of activities?

"Visitors" and "A Night of Frost and a Morning of Mist"

Read the short story, "Visitors," which begins on the next page, and "A Night of Frost and a Morning of Mist," which follows it. Then consider the questions below, which invite you to think about your reactions to the stories and whether you would classify them as "literature" or not.

After Reading

On Your Own

Think about your reactions to the stories you have just read and then write answers to these questions:

- Would you classify the stories as "literature"?
- If so, what reasons would you give?
- If not, why not? What are they, if they aren't literature?

Discuss your answers with a partner, or in small groups, and see if you can arrive at some agreement.

Asking Questions

Now consider the following more general questions about what the term "literature" might mean to you.

In Pairs

Write down as many descriptions and characteristics of literature as you can. You might consider the following as starting points:

- what literature is (what kinds of writing? which authors?);
- how works of literature differ from other kinds of writing;

- the role of literature in society (what is it "for"?);
- why literature is studied;
- the groups of people most interested in literature.

As a Class

After five minutes, contribute your ideas to a chalkboard list for discussion. You will need to refer to this material later, so save your notes. How much agreement or disagreement is there in your class about what literature is and why it is studied? What reasons can you suggest for this?

Visitors

Brian Moon

She saw the mini-bus pass the kitchen window before pulling up on the gravel driveway at the side of the house. It looked like a tradesman's van, with metal panels where the windows would normally be, and ladders strapped to the roof racks. But there was no company name on the side of the van, and she felt her stomach tighten at the unfairness of it. Not again; not so soon!

The knocking was confident but not intimidating. Civilised. She opened the door. There were three men standing on the porch. Two were heavy-set, though well proportioned, and wore clean, neat blue overalls with official insignia on the pockets. One man carried a wicker basket, the other a soft carry-all. The third man, who had knocked at the door and was therefore standing closest to her, had a lighter build. He wore a conservative two-piece suit and was approaching middle age, with dark hair that was just beginning to thin above the forehead. He responded to her appearance at the door by passing pink fingers through his hair in a gesture that suggested tidiness and precision. There was a professional, competent air about him. He looked thoroughly respectable.

"Yes?" she asked.

"Morning madam," he replied affably, professionally. "This is a robbery."

Inside the house, she led them to the lounge. They followed politely, conscious of their movements.

"We had a team through only two weeks ago," she complained.

"Not one of ours, madam. I'm afraid we can't cooperate with the other firms. Competition, you know." He brushed his hair. "You can always put in a complaint."

"Well, where do you want to start?"

"We'd like to put you in the picture first," replied the leader, taking a small notebook from his suit pocket. "We like our customers to know they are dealing with professional people, so I'll just run through the basics." He flipped through the alphabetical tabs on the side of the book, opened to a page covered in neat, pencilled notes and diagrams. He read from it in a confirmatory tone, pausing now and then to check that she understood the details and was happy: "Mrs. Morrison, 42 Wentworth . . ." She nodded; he went on. "Now, we've disconnected your phone at the junction on the corner, and we have a man in the street with a second vehicle just to make sure we won't be surprised by anything unexpected." He gave a small, proud smile. "We disconnected your power on arrival, and of course we'll put that back on as we leave. We know how inconvenient it is to have freezers defrost and so on. The phone, however, is your responsibility, as always. We know that your daughter is at work and won't be back until four at the earliest. We also know that she usually telephones you at eleven, so that it will be . . . ," he checked his watch, briskly, ". . . two and a half hours before she notices the disconnection. Plenty of time. We have, of course, checked out your deliveries, none of which are due this morning." He paused before flipping the notebook shut.

"Yes," she said politely. "You seem very thorough. You must have spent some time checking."

"Two weeks is our normal time frame," he said, finally closing the pad. "A bit unfortunate for you really that we didn't see the other firm come through. It must have been a little over two weeks ago that they called."

"Yes."

The next was asked a little anxiously, as though the wrong answer might introduce a note of unpleasantness. "Did they leave much?"

"Uh, no. They took the lot. But we got the insurance people right away so we've been able to replace most of it."

The man was clearly relieved. He permitted himself another smile and went on.

"Oh good. We hate having to extract a forfeit."

"What is it at the moment?"

"Windows this month," he replied, signalling to one of the other two men, who had been standing patiently by the window. "Six by four or the equivalent. Of course, we break them from the inside so as not to get glass on the furnishings. We can recommend a good glazier, too—real craftsman. I had him do my own place, actually, after we were done over a couple of months back." He was warming to the topic but pulled up short. "Not relevant here, though. Now, do you have any questions?"

"No. It's still rather fresh in my mind," she replied with restrained irony.

"Well then! We'd better get to work."

"Shall I show you through?"

"No, no. You stay right there. We'll take care of it all."

The man with the basket, to whom the leader had gestured, moved to the coffee table and began setting the contents of his hamper onto the polished wood surface. Cup, saucer, thermos, napkins, small glass jars of sugar and milk; and a plate of raisin scones. He moved like a butler; precise, deferential.

"Coffee or tea?"

Sitting with her feet up, hot tea in one hand and a buttered scone in the other, she heard them moving deliberately, methodically through the rooms of the house. The soft clicking of latches punctuated their passage from room to room. Apart from that there was hardly any noise. They spoke only briefly, and she couldn't hear what was said. When she heard them moving up the stairs to the second storey she poured herself another cup. Gradually they worked their way through the second floor, and she marked their progress with mouthfuls of scone and hot tea.

Presently all three men returned to the lounge room. Disregarding her for the moment, the leader spoke to his men.

"Bring the stuff in here and we'll make up the inventory as we load it into the van. It'll be more efficient that way."

The two accomplices nodded and set to work. The leader sat himself down beside the woman, reached for a cup and helped himself to a scone. "Lived in the area long?"

With the coming and going of the men in overalls, a small pile of goods began to build near the entrance hall. Television set; video recorder; kitchen appliances; some jewellery. It didn't take long. After half an hour the leader unseated himself and assessed the haul.

"There, that wasn't so bad," he said reassuringly. "Nothing broken I hope?"

The two others shook their heads.

He turned to the woman. "Will you accompany me on the inspection? We won't entertain claims unless they are notified immediately."

Reluctantly she followed him from room to room, casting a sad glance at the stack of appliances on the floor.

She had to admit that it was a very professional job. There were none of the grubby handprints she'd found on previous occasions; nor were there any shoe marks on the walls. Except for the goods they had taken, everything was in its place. Despite herself, she had to remark on the fact.

"Well, we do have standards to maintain," said the man. "People still remember the old days—a brick through the window, contents strewn about. Mainly it was kids back then, amateurs. People felt like their homes had been violated, like they weren't safe anymore. Gave the profession a very bad name. But things have changed so much since the new legislation. We have to be accredited, audited. It puts the operation on a whole new level."

"Even so," she replied. "I think we'd be better off without . . ."

Imperceptibly, he seemed to stiffen, and she tried to soften it a bit. "Look, you've done a very good job, and you've a right to be proud of it. I'm not attacking you, but I just don't see that it's really necessary." She had let her annoyance show, but he seemed not to take it personally.

"You're talking about jobs, madam, people's livelihood. The country couldn't handle the unemployment. Nationalising robbery was the best thing the government could do in the circumstances. These things are complicated—you can't pin your hopes on simple solutions."

"I suppose so," she replied, not entirely convincingly. They went back downstairs in silence.

It took only a few minutes for them to transfer the haul to the van, itemising each piece as they loaded it. They left her with a copy of the list for insurance purposes. She was only half way through checking it when the car flashed past the window and skidded to a halt on the gravel. An early model panel van, its doors fell open, disgorging a motley collection of young men. There were four of them, dirty, unkempt, and hardly into their teens. They pounded up the steps onto the porch and hammered at the door, rattling the frosted glass.

Her heart pounding expectantly, she opened the door. The oldest of the four leered at her, grinned, and announced himself. "Police, Mrs. Morrison. Understand you've been robbed."

A Night of Frost and a Morning of Mist

Janet Frame

After a night of frost and a morning of mist the day is cloudless. The men of the street have gone to work; the women remain, putting out the milk bottles, shaking the door mats, polishing the windows, dusting the window sills.

Early this morning, a blowfly appeared, the first blowfly of spring, swaggering about in his new navy-blue suit, bumping upon the pane, clamouring. He skated, he buzzed, he walked upside down and sideways, with his feet padded with death. He saw me watching him. He saw me reaching for yesterday's newspaper to fold and creep up and swipe him with it, for he knew that I hated him for appearing from a night of frost and a morning of mist. He was a tiny but swelling speck that would block the sun and plunge the earth into darkness. I knew. I wielded my newspaper.

"Don't kill me," he said, in that small voice used by insects, animals, furniture, who appear in fairy stories and startle people (the woodcutter, his son, the young man lying on the grassy bank in the wood, the servant girl sweeping the bedrooms of the palace) with their cries, "Don't kill me. Help! Help!" He knew, however, that he lived in a modern age when cries for help are ignored when they are made by creatures whose feet are padded with death. So he decided to impress me with his fame.

"Do you know," he said, "that in the Science Museum there is an entire display devoted to my life cycle, with illustrations, models, comprehensive labels? Often my family and I put on our Sunday best and visit the Museum, and may I say that we are received with pleasure?"

The thought of his fame did not deter me from advancing with my folded newspaper. Again he cried, "Help! Help!" Did anyone hear him, anyone engaged in present-day folklore—the builder on the new housing estate, the old man lying in the park in the sun, the junior sweeping the floor of the Beauty Parlour, the man from the Water Board inspecting the manhole covers in the street, the workmen replacing the broken paving stones, the woman with her canvas bag slung over her shoulders going from door to door distributing Free Offers, coupons for soap, frozen peas and spaghetti—those who traditionally receive the confidence of insects, animals, furniture, growing plants? Did they hear? Were they listening? Do they listen carefully as the woodcutter used to do, and the servant girl sweeping the bedrooms of the palace?

"Don't kill me, help, help!"

I struck the newspaper against the windowpane and the bossy fly was dead.

Then I looked out at the almost deserted street, at the early-spring sun shining down on the pavement stones, at the babies lying in their prams outside the houses, at the men digging up the road near the corner, surrounding themselves with bold notices, red flags, lanterns gleaming like rubies. Then outside my own room I glimpsed the tyrant of Grove Hill Road, a heavy-jowled, black-and-white tomcat, the father of most of the kittens in Grove Hill Road, who carries, in his head, maps of dustbins, strategic positions of milk bottles, exact judgements of height of garden and street wall, gate, and the wired street trees that now have tiny pink buds on them, like dolly mixture. The tom has long black whiskers. He was sitting on the gatepost, licking his paws.

Most of the people in the street have been longing to "put him down," which, I understand, is the expression used to describe the sinking activity of dying, and one must beware when tying a stone of lifelessness around anything to make sure one does not also attach the stone to one's own neck—they say.

No one owns the tom; he just appears, and leaves in each house a curl of black and white kittens sucking at a contented suave queen. His reproductions in colour are faultless. But I leaned out of my window.

"Scat!" I said to the tom, hissing at him. "Go on, scat!"

He winked at me.

"First the blowfly, now me," he said. "If the evidence of death does not satisfy you, and the evidence of life satisfies you still less, how in the world are you ever to find satisfaction? Mark my words, you will go to war, my lady."

"Certainly I will go to war," I replied sharply.

And I shut my window and drew a boundary of war, and there I remain to this day, fighting off the armies of life and death which emerge, with the sun, from a night of frost and a morning of mist.

Toward a Definition

When we set out to clarify our understanding of a difficult concept, we often use one or more of the following techniques:

- collecting examples;
- identifying features which all of the examples share;
- identifying the function or value which the concept has in society.

Here is an example of how a simple concept can be defined—in this case, the concept "insect":

Examples of "Insect"	Features	Function or Value
Fly	Three body segments	Pollinates flowers
Ant	Three pairs of legs	Consumes wastes
Termite	An external skeleton	Feeds small animals
Ladybug	Spiracles for breathing	Provides useful chemicals

Of course, this approach assumes that we already have some idea of what we are looking for. (How else would we recognize the examples in the first place?) Its main purpose is to clarify ideas and to help us make predictions and judgments. Armed with this information, for example, we could confidently pass judgment about creatures we have never seen before.

In Pairs

Try using this approach to define "literature." In each column there is a suggested starting point. Complete the chart as fully as you can.

Examples of "Literature"	Features	Function or Value
Plays (e.g., *Hamlet*)	Careful use of language	Entertain

When you have completed your chart, join with another pair to form a group of four. Compare the items you have listed; then discuss the following questions.

- How similar are your charts? Do they seem to offer the same definition of "literature"?
- Which column was the most difficult to complete? Why was this? Which was the easiest? Why?
- Which column seems to best explain what is commonly meant by "literature"?

Report back to the class on your findings.

Testing the Definition

Once we have defined a concept, we can test our definition by using it to classify new items. For example, we can argue that a spider is not an insect because it has eight legs, not six, and we can demonstrate that a wasp is an insect because it has all of the features we expect.

In Groups

Working in groups of four, use your definitions to decide whether the following pieces of writing are "literary" or "nonliterary." For each item:

- state whether it would be regarded as literary or nonliterary by schools and universities in your country;
- state whether it is literary or nonliterary according to your definition;
- comment on how confident you are in your classification.

Samples	School Classification	Your Classification	Comment
Shakespeare's plays			
Daily newspaper			
Harlequin romance novel			
The Bible			
The Koran			
Danielle Steele novel			
Jane Austen novel			
Maya Angelou poem			
Greeting card poems			
Short story by a student			
Script for *The Simpsons*			
Superman comic book			
James Bond novel			

Discuss these points in your group:

- What were the criteria you relied on most in making your decisions?
- Which items were the most difficult to classify? Why?
- Which items were the easiest to classify? Why?
- How much disagreement or agreement is there between the expected school classification and yours? What reasons might there be for this?

What Are the Features of a Literary Work?

Attempts to define literature by listing the features shared by literary works often lead to contradictions. In compiling a list of features, we have to bear two things in mind:

- literary works are of many different types;
- many of the features we associate with literary works can be found in other types of writing as well.

Following is a list of features which are sometimes offered as definitions of literature. How many of them appear on your lists?

Features of a Literary Work
- Contains finely crafted language
- Offers serious themes for consideration
- Is imaginative and creative
- Uses special techniques of writing
- Offers a perceptive view of the world
- Educates as it entertains
- Is generally agreed to have serious merit
- Doesn't have a simple, practical function

One problem with trying to define a concept by listing features is that the terms used are always subject to interpretation. Even in the case of the insect, the meaning of terms such as "leg" and "body segment" is open to debate. The words suggest a clear-cut set of distinctions that we don't really find in the "real world."

This is even more obvious in the case of literature. What is "finely crafted language"? Who decides what is "serious" or "imaginative"? The features listed above are not "objective"; nor are they universally accepted. They are defined differently in different places and at different times by different groups of people.

In Groups

Here are descriptions of three pieces of writing which are clearly not works of literature in the traditional sense.

1. An information leaflet about links between diet and heart disease. It avoids technical language and presents information in an entertaining way. The aim of the leaflet is to contribute to public awareness about heart disease and to suggest lifestyle changes.

2. A popular science book in which a learned physicist gives scientific explanations for the creation of the world and the meaning of human life. To avoid complex language, the scientist relies upon original and clever comparisons to clarify her argument. Humor is used to maintain interest.

3. A book of graffiti collected from all over the world. The material is presented with a minimum of commentary. The examples range from trivial to profound, with comments on social issues often presented in amusing or bawdy language. The editor states that graffiti is an important means of public expression.

For each text, record a check next to the features, listed on the chart below, which might be found in the writing. These are to be group decisions, so discuss each point.

Features	Text 1	Text 2	Text 3
Contains finely crafted language			
Offers serious themes for consideration			
Is imaginative and creative			
Uses special techniques of writing			
Offers a perceptive view of the world			
Educates as it entertains			
Is generally agreed to have serious merit			
Doesn't have a simple, practical function			

■ What do your decisions suggest about the usefulness of this list of literary features?

■ Can you produce a list of features which *all* works of literature share and which will not be found in any other type of writing?

Problems of Definition

The problems faced in defining literature demonstrate that the concept is not as straightforward as our language appears to suggest. The harder we try to pin down exactly what literature is, the more contradictions and confusions we encounter.

Modern theories of literature suggest that "literature," like many other concepts, doesn't really exist at all as a fixed object or category. Rather, what we refer to when we speak of literature has a lot to do with beliefs about what is good writing and what is not.

It is a bit like the concept of weeds. Weeds are not really a type of plant; weeds and plants can't be distinguished from each other on the basis of their features. The term *weeds* simply is used to refer to plants which are not valued in any way—and this varies over time, and from place to place.

Beliefs and Values

It is difficult to build a definition of literature based on a list of features. More useful is a view that sees literature in terms of values and beliefs, as a concept which both springs from and gives rise to certain ways of looking at the world.

On Your Own

Think about a piece of writing which you value: one which has influenced you or been important to you in some way. This might be a fairy tale or children's book; a novel, poem, or story; or a nonfiction work such as an autobiography. Make notes about your choice in the following form:

Title and Author	
Description	(What kind of writing is it? What does it contain?)
Value	(Why is the writing important to you? Which features are responsible for its importance to you? Do you think you will always value it so highly? Why or why not?)

If you can, bring the writing to class to pass around after the following discussion.

In Groups

Form groups of six and take turns reporting to the group on your chosen piece of writing. Using your notes as a guide, explain why it is valuable to you. To begin the discussion, these questions might be asked of each presenter:

- How old were you when you first came across the writing?
- Have your feelings about the writing changed over time?
- Do you know of other people with similar tastes?

As a Class

Compile a chalkboard list of the different types of writing that people have talked about. Make a separate list of the reasons for which people value these pieces of writing. Talk about the following questions:

- How big a range of works is represented?
- Are there types of writing which do not appear? Why might this be?
- How many of the choices would be classed as "literary"? By whom?

On Your Own

Write down your thoughts on these points.

- What might this activity suggest about how writing influences people?
- What could it suggest about people's choices? (How much do they differ? What values or beliefs might they support?)
- What might it suggest about the definition of "literature" which dominates in schools and universities? Does this definition take account of the full range of people's values?

Whose Values?

If decisions about what is and isn't literature are always value judgments, then we are entitled to ask whose values are being supported. Modern theories of literature argue that a society's definitions of literature are shaped by the views of specific groups of people. Since "English Studies" departments first developed in the Arts faculties of British universities, it might be expected that traditional ideas about literature reflect the views of the white, upper-middle-class males who taught at these universities.

Here is a list of people who could be involved in producing, distributing, teaching, and reading the many types of writing created by a particular culture. On your own, rank these people according to how much influence you think they have in deciding what counts as "serious literature." Use "1" to indicate the most influence and "8" the least. Write a brief explanation alongside each ranking. Then, in groups, compare and discuss your rankings.

People	Influence (1–8)	Comment
Writers		
Schoolteachers		
Publishers		
The general public		
"Educated" readers		
University professors		
Critics		
Booksellers		

The Question of Taste

In the 1920s, a young lecturer in English at Cambridge University, I. A. Richards, set out to study the "literary judgment" of his first-year students. He presented the students with a range of poems, minus their titles and authors' names. Richards wondered whether his students could demonstrate good judgment without these vital "clues."

He published the results in a book titled *Practical Criticism*. Many students criticized the work of famous literary figures and praised the writing of unknown authors. Richards concluded that many of his students had poorly developed tastes. He assumed that the works of great authors had qualities which clearly distinguished them from other writing and that his students needed to have their reading skills refined so they could see these qualities.

On Your Own

Following is a selection of poems without titles or authors' names. Read and make notes about each in response to these questions:

- ◼ What is the subject matter of the poem?
- ◼ What poetic "techniques" can you find? (Consider figurative language, unusual word order, metaphor and simile, and so on.)
- ◼ Which techniques seem most effective to you?
- ◼ What appears to be the theme, or general meaning, of the poem?
- ◼ What is your personal response to the poem? What factors have influenced your response?

Poem 1

Why are we here?
What's it all about?
Here one minute and
Gone the next.
What does it matter
What I want to be when
I grow up?
It all ends the same.
People live.
Then they die.
But the universe rolls
On.

Poem 2

It's a nice day for dying
Death of a mother
"You can come in now"
Slap in the face
Relationships
Building
Battle
Hunger
Softly we tread.

Poem 3

As I sd to my
friend, because I am
always talking,—John, I
sd, which was not his
name, the darkness sur-
rounds us, what

can we do against
it, or else shall we &
why not, buy a goddam big car,

drive, he sd, for
christ's sake, look
out where yr going.

Poem 4

Tempus Fugit!*

Progress would be good
if only it would stop.

You know what I hate?

Having children!

* (Tempus Fugit: time flies)

Poem 5

Beauty
is a fat black woman
walking in the fields
pressing a breezed
hibiscus
to her cheek
while the sun lights up.

   Beauty
   is a fat black woman
   riding the waves
   drifting in happy oblivion
   while the sea turns back
   to hug her shape.

Poem 6

It feels just like
he's gone down the road
for a gin and tonic.
I never thought I'd feel this way.
My emotions never showed.

Clearing out his things
felt just like packing
for a holiday.

Ranking the Poems

When you have answered the questions for each poem, rank the poems in an order of quality, from best to worst. Briefly explain the reasons for your rankings. In groups, compare the rankings you have given to the poems. If there are differences, discuss them and try to create an agreed-upon group ranking. Record the results on a chart similar to the one below.

Poems	Personal Ranking	Group Ranking	Comment
Poem 1			
Poem 2			
Poem 3			
Poem 4			
Poem 5			
Poem 6			

Once you have arrived at a group ranking, turn to page 29 for details of each poem's title and authorship, and then discuss these questions:

■ Are you surprised by any of the details of titles and authors? If so, which ones, and why? Did you predict that some were "found" poems?

■ What might this activity suggest about the following: the difficulty of judging literary quality? the argument that literary judgment must be taught? the difficulty of defining what literature is?

■ What role does reading play in deciding which pieces of writing are "literary"? Can we choose to read in a "literary" way? Is there anything that cannot be read in this way?

■ If you were "fooled" by some of the examples, what does this prove: that literature doesn't really exist? that you haven't yet learned how to judge poetry properly? something else?

One of the interesting things about I. A. Richards's experiment was that it showed how values and beliefs which seem obvious to one person might not be obvious to others. Richards didn't seem to be aware that his literary judgment was based on a particular set of beliefs about life in general.

English Literature

The work of black writers traditionally has been excluded from the category of "English literature" but is now being published in countries such as the United States, Canada, Great Britain, and Australia. On the next page are two such poems: by Eva Johnson, an Aboriginal Australian writer born at Daly River in the Northern Territory and Linton Kwesi Johnson, a Jamaican-born writer living in Great Britain.

Weevilly Porridge

Eva Johnson

Weevilly porridge I'm going insane
Weevilly porridge gonna wreck my brain
Stir in treacle, make'em taste sweet
Put'em on stove, turn'em up heat
Milk from powder tin, milk from goat
Weevilly porridge, pour'em down throat.

MmmMmm, mission food, send'em from heaben must be good
MmmMmm, mission food, send'em from heaben must be good

Nebba mind the weevil, nebba mind the taste
Missionary she bin say, "don't you waste'
Weevilly porridge, make'em pretty strong
Spread'em on Dampa can't go wrong. (Dampa: bread-like food)

Bless'em little weevil, bless'em little me
We bin lunga trick'em just you see
Catch'em little weevil, put'em in the tea
Only fullah drink'em up missionary.

Protector He bin call on us give us daily ration
Cook'em up plenty food for Him, together we bin mash'em
Weevils in the sago, weevils in the rice
Protector He bin lunga saying—Mmmm, taste nice.

Yout Scene

Linton Kwesi Johnson

last satdey
I neva dey pan no faam
so I decide fe tek a walk
doun a BRIXTON,
an see wha gwane. (gwane: going on)

de bredrin dem stan-up
outside a HIP CITY,
as usual, a look pretty;

dem a laaf big laaf
dem a talk dread talk
dem a shuv an shuffle dem feet,
soakin in de sweet MUSICAL BEAT.

but when nite come
policeman run dem dung; (dung: down)
beat dem dung a grung, (grung: ground)
kick dem ass,
sen dem pass justice
to prison walls of gloom.
but de bredda dem a scank; (scank: escape)
dem naw rab bank;
is packit dem a pick
an is woman dem a lick
an is run dem a run when de WICKED come. (Wicked: police)

In Groups

Many aspects of these poems—including the subject matter and the use of "non-standard" dialects—challenge traditional conventions of "English verse." Choose one of the poems; then work together to fill in the following chart. In the left-hand column, record the traditional view of literature, as you see it, on the aspects indicated. In the right-hand column, explain how poems such as "Weevilly Porridge" and "Yout Scene" challenge the tradition of "English literature."

Traditional View		Modern View
The "appropriate" language for poetry.	1	The "appropriate" language for poetry.
The "appropriate" subject matter for poetry.	2	The "appropriate" subject matter for poetry.
Who is qualified to write poetry.	3	Who is qualified to write poetry.
Who is most likely to read and enjoy poetry.	4	Who is most likely to read and enjoy poetry.

preconceptions

Share your group's answers with other class members. The headings "Traditional View" and "Modern View" are, of course, simplifications. In any age there are always competing views on every subject. What is meant by such headings is the *dominant*, or most influential or powerful, view in a particular time and place.

For Discussion

The increasing diversity of published writing raises the question of how "literature" has been classified in the past and how it is to be classified now—by country of origin, for example, or author's race, or not at all. Is "English literature" that which has been written in England, in the "English language," or by "English" people? How is it possible to define who or what is "English"? Perhaps terms such as "English literature" should be done away with. What do you think?

Challenging Beliefs

In general, belief in the individual has dominated literary study since about 1800. But since the 1960s the balance has started to shift. Many modern theories of literature, including the theory on which this book is based, examine works of literature in terms of social structures. One of the reasons for this shift is that some people have successfully challenged the beliefs on which traditional approaches to literature were based.

Traditional Beliefs

Here are some traditional beliefs about literature which still have influence among some groups of people:

- Literature offers us the best thoughts of the best minds.
- Literature does more than entertain; it teaches us what it means to be human.
- Literature is language used in its highest form.
- Literature offers us words of goodness, truth, and beauty.
- Literary works are writings of the highest quality.
- Literary classics will live forever.
- Appreciation of literature is a sign of intelligence.
- You cannot love literature and be a bad person.

If these statements are investigated, we can see that they are based on assumptions about language, society, and what it is to be a human being. Some of these assumptions are that:

- literary works are different from other kinds of writing;
- some forms of language are better than others;
- some thoughts (and minds) are worthier than others;
- goodness, truth, and beauty mean the same thing to everyone;
- all people share a common "human" nature.

These are ideas which can be questioned. Consider the statement that literature offers "the best thoughts of the best minds." It might be argued that this statement assumes (1) that literature can offer us a writer's thoughts; (2) that some people's thoughts are better than others; and (3) that literary works are those which contain the best thoughts.

Each of these assumptions can be challenged. The simplest way is to turn the assumptions into questions and then state an opposing view, like this:

1. Assumption: Literature can offer us a writer's thoughts.

   Can literature offer us a writer's thoughts? Some theorists argue that we can never know whether the meanings we make when we read are the same as those which the writer had in mind. If this is so, then the "thoughts" we seem to find in works of literature might be ours—or those which society expects us to find—and not the author's at all.

2. Assumption: Some people's thoughts are better than others.

   Are some people's thoughts better than others? Perhaps the value of a person's thoughts can be measured only according to the dominant beliefs of his or her society. In some cultures, it is good scholarship to copy the work of other writers. In other societies, this practice is illegal. What is "good" depends upon time, place, and cultural beliefs.

3. Assumption: Literary works contain the best thoughts.

   Do literary works contain the "best" thoughts? Who is in a position to judge this? It may be that literary works are simply those which reinforce the ideas of a particular group in our society. Not everyone will share these ideas and judge them to be the best.

In Groups

Try challenging the assumptions which are supported by two or three of these statements about literature.

- Literature teaches us about the world and how we should live.
- Literary classics will live forever.
- You cannot love literature and be a bad person.
- Literature is language used in its highest form.
- Literary works are writings of the highest quality.

Stage one: For each statement, make a list of the beliefs, or assumptions, which are implied by what has been said. Stage two: For each set of beliefs, challenge the assumptions by turning them into questions and stating an opposing view. Note the points raised in discussion using these headings: Statement, Assumptions, and Challenges.

In Pairs

Refer back to the definition of literature which you wrote at the beginning of this chapter. Swap your notes with a partner and do the following: (1) list the assumptions which underlie your partner's definition; (2) challenge the assumptions by writing questions under the definition. Return the work and discuss:

- What assumptions in your definition were you not aware of?
- How similar are your assumptions to those of people sitting near you? What might be the reasons for this? (Consider the influence of education, friendships, family background, gender, and so on.)

If you don't have your own definitions available, work through the activity using this definition, written by a student of your age.

> Literature, to me, means serious writing. Literature is deeper than the kind of things we read just for fun. You have to think about it, whereas other books just get read and then forgotten. Literature is usually harder to read, too. You have to be more intelligent to understand it because you have to be able to find the author's themes and understand how he or she uses language. Literature is a valuable thing to study because it teaches us about life and how to behave properly in society.

- How closely does this definition match the traditional idea of literature?
- Indicate aspects of the student's definition which are called into question by the ideas you have been examining in this chapter.

For Discussion

Discuss the kind of writing which might be judged "literary" if students like you had the power to challenge traditional definitions of what is literary and what is not. Would it necessarily be different? Why or why not?

"To a Butterfly" and "Good-Bye Worn Out Morris 1000"

The poems which follow were written by people who claim to draw their subject matter from "ordinary life." Pam Ayres is a popular British writer. She gives live performances of her poetry on stage, in a dialect which some would label "rural English."

William Wordsworth was an influential writer who lived in England from 1770 to 1850. He is still regarded as a "serious poet" by many teachers and university professors. Wordsworth published a collection of poetry titled *Lyrical Ballads*, and in the preface he argued that poets should focus their attention on the language of "ordinary" people.

Read the poems with this question in mind: Why is it that one of these writers is widely regarded as having produced "literature," while the other is widely regarded as having produced "light entertainment"?

To a Butterfly

William Wordsworth

I've watched you now a full half-hour,
Self-poised upon that yellow flower;
And, little Butterfly! indeed
I know not if you sleep or feed.
How motionless! and then
What joy awaits you, when the breeze
Hath found you out among the trees,
And calls you forth again!

This plot of orchard-ground is ours;
My trees they are, my Sister's flowers;
Here rest your wings when they are weary;
Here lodge as in a sanctuary!
Come often to us, fear no wrong;
Sit near us on the bough!
We'll talk of sunshine and of song,
And summer days, when we were young;
Sweet childish days, that were as long
As twenty days are now.

Good-Bye Worn Out Morris 1000

Pam Ayres

Oh love, you got no poke left
I didn't want to say,
It seems we are outmoded,
Much too slow, and in the way.
You know how much I love you;
I'd repair you in a flash
But I haven't got the knowledge
And I haven't got the cash.

There is rust all round your headlamps,
I could push through it if I tried
My pot of paint can't cure it
"Cause it's from the other side.
All along your sides and middle
You are turning rusty brown,
Though you took me ninety thousand miles
And never let me down.

Not the snapping of the fan belt
Nor the blowing of a tyre
Nor the rattling of a tappet
And nor did you misfire.

All your wheels stayed on the corners
And your wipers on the screen
Though I didn't do much for you
And I never kept you clean.

All your seats are upholstered
And foam rubber specks the floor.
You were hit by something else once
And I cannot shut the door.
But it's not these things that grieve me
Or the money that I spent,
For you were my First-driven,
Ninety thousand miles we went.

I could buy a bright and new car
And go tearing round the town
A BGT! A Morgan!
(With the hood all battened down).
But as I leave the scrapyard,
Bangers piled up to the skies,
Why do your rusty headlamps
Look like sad, reproachful eyes?

On Your Own

Here are four arguments which might be made about the poems you have just read:

1. Wordsworth's poem is better than Ayres's.

2. Ayres's poem is better than Wordsworth's.

3. These are different types of poetry and so cannot be compared; both are successful examples of their type.

4. There are no absolute measures of quality, so it is not possible to say that one poem is better or worse than another.

Pick the answer closest to your own and then note all of the supporting points you can think of. When you have done this, make a second set of notes explaining why you reject the other arguments.

In Groups

Form groups in which there are representatives (if possible) of arguments 1, 2, 3, and 4 above; let each person present his or her case, and then discuss objections to each position. Try to arrive at a consensus of opinion about the issues.

As a Class

- Share with the class some of the most interesting or challenging questions raised in your discussion.
- Within the literary "establishment," Wordsworth rates more highly than Pam Ayres. Discuss which of the following might account for this.

The sound of the language
The writer's sex
The subject matter
The age of the writing
The use of literary "technique" (specify)
The mode of presentation
The writer's place in literary tradition
Other reasons (specify)

"Edgar and Emma: A Tale"

Use the following story by Jane Austen to think about the criteria you have learned to use for judging the merit of a piece of writing. A major figure in traditional literary studies, Austen wrote such famous novels as *Pride and Prejudice, Sense and Sensibility, Mansfield Park,* and *Emma.* She lived in England from 1775 to 1817. What is your opinion of "Edgar and Emma: A Tale"?

Edgar and Emma: A Tale _____

Jane Austen

Chapter 1

"I cannot imagine," said Sir Godfrey to his lady, "why we continue in such deplorable lodgings as these, in a paltry market-town, while we have three good houses of our own situated in some of the finest parts of England, and perfectly ready to receive us!"

"I'm sure Sir Godfrey," replied Lady Marlow, "it has been much against my inclination that we have staid here so long; or why we should ever have come at all indeed, has been to me a wonder, as none of our houses have been in the least want of repair."

"Nay my dear," answered Sir Godfrey, "you are the last person who ought to be displeased with what was always meant as a compliment to you; for you cannot but be sensible of the very great inconvenience your daughters and I have been put to, during the two years we have remained crowded in these lodgings in order to give you pleasure."

"My dear," replied Lady Marlow, "How can you stand and tell such lies, when you very well know that it was merely to oblige the girls and you, that I left a most commodious house situated in a most agreeable neighbourhood, to live two years cramped up in lodgings three pair of stairs high, in a smokey and unwholesome town, which has given me a continual fever and almost thrown me into a consumption."

As, after a few more speeches on both sides, they could not determine which was the most to blame, they prudently laid aside the debate, and having packed up their clothes and paid their rent, they set out the next morning with their two daughters for their seat in Sussex.

Sir Godfrey and Lady Marlow were indeed very sensible people and tho' (as in this instance) like many other sensible people, they sometimes did a foolish thing, yet in general their actions were guided by prudence and regulated by discretion.

After a journey of two days and a half they arrived at Marlhurst in good health and high spirits; so overjoyed were they all to inhabit again a place, they had left with mutual regret for two years, that they ordered the bells to be rung and distributed ninepence among the ringers.

Chapter 2

The news of their arrival being quickly spread throughout the country, brought them in a few days visits of congratulation from every family in it.

Amongst the rest came in inhabitants of Wilmot Lodge, a beautiful villa not far from Marlhurst. Mr. Wilmot was the representative of a very ancient family and possessed besides his paternal estate, a considerable share in a lead mine and a ticket in the lottery. His lady was an agreeable woman. Their children were too numerous to be particularly described; it is sufficient to say that in general they were virtuously inclined and not given to any wicked ways. Their family being too large to accompany them in every visit, they took nine with them alternately. When their coach stopped at Sir Godfrey's door, the Miss Marlows' hearts throbbed in the eager expectation of once more beholding a family so dear to them. Emma the youngest (who was more particularly interested in their arrival, being attached to their eldest son) continued at her dressing-room window in anxious hopes of seeing the young Edgar descend from the carriage.

Mr. and Mrs. Wilmot with their three eldest daughters first appeared—Emma began to tremble. Robert, Richard, Ralph and Rodolphus followed—Emma turned pale. Their two youngest girls were lifted from the coach—Emma sunk breathless on the sofa. A footman came to announce to her the arrival of company; her heart was too full to contain its afflictions. A confidante was necessary. In Thomas she hoped to experience a faithful one—for one she must have and Thomas was the only one at hand. To him she unbosomed herself without restraint and after owning her passion for young Wilmot, requested his advice in what manner she should conduct herself in the melancholy disappointment under which she laboured.

Thomas, who would gladly have been excused from listening to her complaint, begged leave to decline giving any advice concerning it, which much against her will, she was obliged to comply with.

Having dispatched him therefore with many injunctions of secrecy, she descended with a heavy heart into the parlour, where she found the good party seated in a social manner round a blazing fire.

Chapter 3

Emma had continued in the parlour some time before she could summon up sufficient courage to ask Mrs. Wilmot after the rest of her family; and when she did, it was in so low, so faltering a voice that no one knew she spoke. Dejected by the ill success of her first attempt she made no other, till on Mrs. Wilmot's desiring one of the girls to ring the bell for their carriage, she stepped across the room and seizing the string said in a resolute manner.

"Mrs. Wilmot, you do not stir from this house till you let me know how all the rest of your family do, particularly your eldest son."

They were all greatly surprised by such an unexpected address and the more so, on account of the manner in which it was spoken; but Emma, who would not be again disappointed, requesting an answer, Mrs. Wilmot made the following eloquent oration.

"Our children are all extremely well but at present most of them from home. Amy is with my sister Clayton. Sam at Eton. David with his Uncle John. Jem and Will at Winchester. Kitty at Queen's Square. Ned with his grandmother. Hetty and Patty in a convent at Brussells. Edgar at college, Peter at nurse, and all the rest (except the nine here) at home."

It was with difficulty that Emma could refrain from tears on hearing of the absence of Edgar; she remained however tolerably composed till the Wilmots were gone when having no check to the overflowings of her grief, she gave free vent to them, and retiring to her own room, continued in tears the remainder of her life.

On Your Own

Make a detailed plan of your answer to the question, "What is your opinion of this story?" List all of the strengths and weaknesses of the writing, as you perceive them, and be prepared to give examples to clarify or justify the comments you make.

In Groups

When you have exhausted your ideas, share your evaluation and your reasoning with other students in a small-group discussion. Use a chart similar to the one below to record your group's evaluation of some aspects or elements of the story.

Story Element	Evaluation
Style of the prose	Long-winded and wordy Clear and precise Immature Effective Other:
Speech of the characters	Unrealistic Accurate Believable Other:
Behavior of Emma	Understandable Typical Very odd Interesting Other:
Characterization	Clumsy Engrossing Skillful Tedious Other:
Plot	Captivating Nonsensical Dull Effective Other:
Subject matter	Interesting Too simple Dated Too complex Other:

As a Class

After discussing your evaluations, consider your responses in terms of:

- your ideas of what is normal behavior;
- the kind of language you feel comfortable with;
- your expectations of what makes a good story;
- your cultural background.

For example, if you found the language wordy and dull, does it mean that you have "poor taste," or does it suggest that the story is poorly written? Alternatively, what might such a criticism suggest about concepts such as "literary genius," "classic texts," and "unchanging values"? What have you evaluated in this activity?

- ■ The writing?
- ■ The writer?
- ■ Your taste?
- ■ Your culture?
- ■ The gap between Austen's world and yours?
- ■ All of these things?

How does this complicate your initial assumptions about the study of literature?

Summary

Decisions about which pieces of writing a society considers literary are matters of value judgment. There is no "objective" list of features which can be used as a checklist, no test which can be applied to detect "literary quality." Instead, a piece of writing must always be examined against its social background. No piece of writing exists in a vacuum. Every text is caught up in a network of relationships between:

- ■ the writer who set it down on paper;
- ■ the readers who read it;
- ■ the cultural contexts within which writers and readers live.

This means that "literature" is not a set of books which are somehow special. It is a set of activities in which people engage. It is about writing, reading, and making judgments according to certain beliefs and practices. So, instead of studying a piece of writing in isolation, we must study it as one component of a larger network. If we take this view, we will find ourselves asking questions like these about the texts we study:

- ■ Does the writing try to offer the reader a particular view of the world, by silencing or suppressing other possibilities, or is it open to being interpreted in a variety of ways by people with a variety of beliefs and values?
- ■ What possible readings might people from different times, places, and social backgrounds construct from the text?
- ■ What functions do these readings of the text serve? Do they maintain or challenge particular ways of thinking?
- ■ To which features of the writing do people pay most attention ? Why?

On a more general level, a study of literary texts leads to questions like these:

- Are there features which distinguish different types of writing?
- What kinds of judgments do readers make about what they read?
- On what basis are these judgments made?
- Can we ever say that some pieces of writing are better than others?
- What effects do texts have on readers, writers, and society?
- How much of texts' meanings are constructed by the writers, the readers, and the societies in which they write and read?
- Why do some texts tend to be valued over others?
- How and why do readings of texts change?

In the chapters that follow—and in your course of study—you will search for answers to these and other questions.

Summary Checklist

To check your understanding of the ideas argued in this chapter, use the following checklist. In the first column indicate those statements which are supported or implied by the chapter. Use "T" or "F" to indicate true or false. In the second column, record your opinion for each statement. When you have made your responses, work in groups of four to discuss the results:

- Check that you are all in agreement about which statements are supported or implied by the chapter. In cases of disagreement, go back to the relevant section and discuss the material.
- Compare your responses and discuss any differences which arise.

Statements	Chapter	You
1. Writing that stands the test of time must have some genuine relevance to everyone.		
2. There are no absolute, unchanging measures of what is good or bad in writing.		
3. Judgments about the value of a piece of writing always reflect the beliefs and values of the speaker; there are no impartial measures of quality.		
4. "Found poems" prove that literature is really a matter of how we read, not how we write.		
5. The study of literature must involve some study of the culture and society; it is not enough to read the works themselves.		

Sources of Poems on Page 14

Four of the poems are "real," having been written as poetry. The other two are "found poems": pieces of writing which we can read in poetic ways even though they were not written as poetry. Only poems 3, 5, and 6 are by "established" writers. Here is a list of the poems' origins:

Poem 1: Poem by an unknown student.
Poem 2: Table of contents from a book of student poems.
Poem 3: "I Know a Man" by Robert Creeley.
Poem 4: Table of contents from a book of student stories.
Poem 5: "Beauty" by Grace Nichols.
Poem 6: "Rest in Peace" by Alix Chmelnitzky.

2 Reading "Literary" Texts

■ How can the act of reading construct meaning from texts?
■ What are reading practices?
■ Where do reading practices come from?
■ What are "gaps" and "silences" in texts?
■ How can readers challenge dominant or conventional readings of a text?

Texts as Cultural Artifacts

Like cars, computers, clothing, and other consumer goods, written texts are products of culture; as cultural artifacts, these things are made to fit into people's lives and to support certain ways of thinking and acting. Also like manufactured goods, texts are created as a result of a process: raw materials are gathered, designs are consulted, guidelines are followed, the final product is distributed, and consumers buy and make use of the article. How this process works in the case of, say, a motor car or a piece of clothing may seem reasonably obvious, but what are the factors involved in producing a novel or a poem?

In Groups

Working in groups of four, create a flowchart or diagram which shows your idea of the "manufacturing process" for a "work of literature." Your diagram should explain the following:

■ what the raw materials are and where they come from;
■ where the process begins and ends, if it does;
■ the roles of writers;
■ the roles of readers;
■ where the meanings of a text come from;
■ how beliefs and values in different cultures influence the process. (Where, for example, do social institutions such as education fit in?)

When you have finished, display your diagram on a large sheet of paper and explain to the class how it works. Keep this material for later use.

The Traditional Model

The idea that works of literature can be treated as cultural artifacts is fairly recent. This is because the literary tradition of the past two hundred years has regarded such writing as the result of individual creative genius. The "romantic" view of writing diagrams the activity this way:

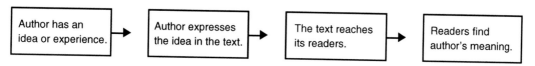

This approach, which begins the process with the author and ends it with the reader, rests on a number of assumptions. It assumes that:

- writers put original ideas into texts;
- a text contains the same ideas forever;
- readers extract meaning from the text;
- writers and readers are individuals acting alone.

In this view, writing is individual expression, and what is expressed is the writer's unique experience of the world. But these assumptions can be challenged by considering what happens when people read literary texts.

"Song: That Women Are but Mens Shaddowes"

On your own, read the following poem by an Elizabethan poet, Ben Jonson (ca. 1572–1637). Poems of this type were often structured around an interesting or peculiar comparison. This technique was used by Jonson, John Donne (1573–1631), George Herbert (1593–1633), and others of the so-called "metaphysical" school.

Song: That Women Are but Mens Shaddowes _____

Ben Jonson

Follow a shaddow, it still flies you;
Seem to flye it, it will pursue:
So court a mistris, shee denyes you;
Let her alone, shee will court you.
Say, are not women truely, then,
Stil'd but the shaddowes of us men?
At morne, and even, shades are longest;
At noone, they are short, or none:

So men at weakest, they are strongest,
But grant us perfect, they're not knowne. (perfect: full grown)
Say, are not women truely, then,
Stil'd but the shaddowes of us men? (stil'd: styled)

Use the table below to explore the comparison between women and shadows in the poem above. Some examples have been completed to get you started. The numbers in brackets refer to line numbers in the poem.

Shadows	Women
Flee when chased (1)	Play hard-to-get when courted
Follow when run from (2)	
Are long in the morning (7)	Are powerful when men are very young
Are long in the evening (7)	
Are smallest in full sun (8)	

Write down your thoughts on which of the following might be read as the main point of the poem, that is, as its "subject." Give reasons for your choice(s).

a. The relative importance of women and men?

b. How women behave when courted?

c. A warning to men about the inconstancy of women?

d. The comparison between women and shadows?

e. The "fickle nature" of women?

f. The pomposity of men?

g. The superior reasoning power of men?

h. Advice on how to succeed in love?

How might male and female readers react differently to some of the meanings produced by these readings of the subject of the poem? Why?

In Groups

Share your answers; then read the passage below and discuss the questions which follow:

In Ben Jonson's day, the dominant reading of the "subject" of this poem was the interesting comparison between women and shadows. The poem was praised because it was read as making this unusual comparison work at a number of points. Poems based on unusual comparisons seemed to be generally much admired. The fact that this comparison rested on the assumption that women were men's inferiors appears to have been "invisible" to most readers, because a dominant view of the time was that women were lesser beings. Similarly, the fact that the poem assumes all readers to be male (it addresses itself very clearly to men) apparently was not considered unusual.

- How do the poem's possible modern meanings compare with the former dominant "meaning" summarized above?
- How might the meanings of this poem constructed by different groups of readers differ today?
- What does this suggest about the idea that poems contain a single meaning which stays the same forever for all readers?
- Are there groups in society today who would still read the poem without (a) challenging its former dominant meaning, that is, that women are lesser beings, or (b) finding it offensive? (Is, for example, any particular group in your class jokingly agreeing with the former dominant reading of the poem?) If so, discuss whether this indicates that poems can have more than one meaning at any one time, and how readers might choose between meanings.
- How do your answers to these questions complicate the study of literary texts?

Dominant and Marginalized Ideas

Just because it is possible to find many poems of this sort in books of poetry doesn't mean one should assume that everyone in Jonson's day accepted this way of thinking about men and women. In every age, there are groups of people who challenge and reject the prevailing views. It is important to distinguish between those ideas which are most powerfully or officially promoted, and those which are suppressed or ignored. The following terms are helpful.

- **Dominant ideas:** these are ideas promoted by official institutions such as the law and schooling. They may not be accepted by everyone in society, but they are important in maintaining certain power structures.
- **Marginalized or subordinate ideas:** these are ideas held by people who may not have access to positions of power. The existence of these ideas is often denied or ignored by dominant institutions.

Meaning and Cultural Context

If other readings of Ben Jonson's poem are possible now, this is not because the words on the page have changed. It is because changes in the dominant ideas and practices of the cultures in which the poem is read have made different readings possible.

Jonson's poem may have suited the dominant ideas of the time in which it was written, but we can be sure that even then some people would have challenged it. Why is it that we have little record of such challenges but lots of poems which express a dominant view of men, women, and their relationships?

As a Class

How might each of the following factors help to explain the preservation of Jonson's poem and the disappearance of poems, many of them by women, which might have challenged dominant ideas? Could it be the fact that:

- Jonson is a male writer?
- publishing companies have traditionally been owned and run by men?
- men controlled the wealth and finances necessary to produce books?
- most teachers in universities traditionally have been men?
- most families educated only sons, not daughters?
- women traditionally have lacked financial independence?

Reading Practices

The reading of any text is guided by a set of culturally determined "reading conventions" or "reading practices." These are ways of reading which are constructed by, and in turn support, social structures. Some of the structures which influence the way in which literary works are created and used include: the family, the education system, the church, the law, and the media.

These social structures do not necessarily make explicit statements about how people should read. But they are powerful influences on how people see the world. In modern western societies, these institutions have all promoted the idea of authority. Through them people learn the value of being obedient, of recognizing power and superiority.

In Groups

For each of the social structures listed below, describe some of the ways in which the acceptance of authority is taught. An example is given.

Institution	Authority Figures
Church	Authority figures include a god or gods, as well as officials such as priests. Followers accept the authority of sacred writings and the word of the officials.
Family	
School	
The law	
The media	

Guarantees?

In each of these cases, the function of the authority figure is to try to guarantee a particular meaning or set of meanings as *the* meaning of things. The truth of sacred writings is "guaranteed" by their presentation as the word of a god. The truth of television news is "guaranteed" by the newsreader's authoritative presentation.

Some ways of reading or kinds of reading practices try to guarantee or fix certain meanings (that support dominant views of the world) by constructing a reading of a text, a reading which is claimed to be *the* meaning of the text, unchangeable over time and the same for all groups of readers.

The statements below summarize a range of opposing ways of reading, or reading practices. Discuss the statements and then try to match each one with its opposite. You may decide that some statements have more than one match.

Reading Practices	
1. Reading "between the lines" to find the author's meaning.	a. Making visible the gaps and silences in a text.
2. Accepting the interpretation given by "experts."	b. Looking for contradictions in the text.
3. Looking for a single "theme" or meaning in a text.	c. Exploring the range of possible meanings for a text.
4. Accepting the reading apparently invited by the text.	d. Pointing to "formula" features of the text.
5. Looking for the "ring of truth" in a text.	e. Questioning the text and the possible readings it supports.
6. Finding proof of the author's originality.	f. Analyzing how a reading is produced and what values it supports.
7. Assuming that the text makes sense.	g. Reading for evidence of a text's connections with other texts.

Challenging Tradition

Modern literary theories are exploring ways in which readers can challenge the traditional readings of literary texts. They argue that readings of a text are not simply interpretations of what is there; rather, these readings are constructed in support of the values and beliefs of particular groups of people. Traditional or dominant readings therefore work to silence groups with alternative beliefs and values.

Gaps, Silences, and Contradictions in Literature

One way of challenging the apparent authority of a text is to adopt reading practices which look for contradictions, gaps, or silences in the text. Another is to analyze the ways in which readings are constructed.

Traditional reading practices assume literary texts to be "perfectly" complete and unified. But modern theories of reading suggest that this sense of completeness is produced by the reading, not the text. Literary texts *seem* self-contained and complete because they deal with knowledge that the reader already has. Because of this, it can be said that even those texts a reader has not seen before are "already read."

"The Eagle"

Read the following poem by Alfred, Lord Tennyson on your own; then write about the impression you have of the eagle. What kind of creature is it? What qualities does it appear to have?

The Eagle _____

Alfred, Lord Tennyson

He clasps the crag with crooked hands;
Close to the sun in lonely lands,
Ringed with the azure world, he stands.
The wrinkled sea beneath him crawls;
He watches from his mountain walls,
And like a thunderbolt he falls.

In Groups

Before you compare your written responses, work through these activities.

1. List all of the eagle's physical features described in the poem.

2. List all of the words in the poem that describe the eagle's actions.

3. List all of the features of the eagle's environment described in the poem.

   Discuss your findings, using the following questions as a guide:

■ Why is there so little information given in the poem about the eagle?
■ How many actions described in the poem are unique to eagles or birds?
■ What could this poem mean to readers who do not know what an eagle is? Could they be sure that the poem was about a bird?

   Now share your initial written responses to the poem.

■ How much of what you wrote was based on information from the poem, and how much was based on your knowledge of eagles and what they are associated with, or stand for, in your culture?
■ Where has most of the "meaning" come from? Is it from the text; that is, from the words on the page—or from the reading? If it is from the reading, can you say how?

■ Would a reader necessarily produce the dominant reading of this poem (that it is about an eagle) if the title were withheld? What does this suggest about the relative importance of textual features in triggering a specific reading for this poem? Which appears to be most influential here, the title or the "body" of the poem?

Other Readings?

Now read the poem without its title. What other possible readings of the poem might there be? What, other than an eagle, could the poem be describing?

He clasps the crag with crooked hands;
Close to the sun in lonely lands,
Ringed with the azure world, he stands.
The wrinkled sea beneath him crawls;
He watches from his mountain walls,
And like a thunderbolt he falls.

The poem is printed below with a few changes in the pronouns. Read the poem and, in pairs, suggest possible readings of the altered text. What might the poem be describing? Share these readings in a class discussion.

She clasps the crag with crooked hands;
Close to the sun in lonely lands,
Ringed with the azure world, she stands.
The wrinkled sea beneath her crawls;
She watches from her mountain walls,
And like a thunderbolt she falls.

Where Are the Readings Coming From?

Here is one student's reading of the altered poem above, which was presented without its title.

I think this is a poem about a witch or hag. I can't be sure what she is doing, but I think she might be climbing up a craggy cliff to get to a castle or some kind of lair. I think she is a witch because her hands are crooked and gnarled, and because she gazes down from the mountain with a stare that makes the sea crawl. Also, she falls like a thunderbolt, as if she has magical powers of some kind. Or she may have been struck down as punishment for a wicked deed. The woman in the poem is powerful but evil. The reader is made to feel anxious as he or she looks up in his or her imagination, waiting to see what she will do.

■ Are there any points in this paragraph which match your reading of the altered poem? If so, discuss these points in your group.
■ Many people produce readings of the altered poem which contrast sharply with their readings of the original. Can these changes be fully explained by such small alterations to the text? If not, where are the readings coming from?

■ If a text's meanings are constructed, at least in part, by filling gaps in the text with ideas that are already available in the reader's culture, what might this activity suggest about dominant attitudes of your culture toward women and men?

Silences and *Hard Times*

Texts not only exhibit gaps; they are also silent about certain issues. Because the raw materials of a text are drawn from ideas which circulate in a culture, texts share in promoting the values and beliefs of dominant groups. This may be the case even if a particular author aims to challenge a dominant way of thinking.

The following extract is from Charles Dickens's novel *Hard Times*. Read the passage carefully, and then complete the activities which follow.

It was a town of red brick, or of brick that would have been red if the smoke and ashes had allowed it; but as matters stood it was a town of unnatural red and black like the painted face of a savage. It was a town of machinery and tall chimneys, out of which interminable serpents of smoke trailed themselves for ever, and never got uncoiled. It had a black canal in it, and a river that ran purple with ill-smelling dye, and vast piles of buildings full of windows where there was a rattling and a trembling all day long, and where the piston of the steam-engine worked monotonously up and down, like the head of an elephant in a state of melancholy madness. It contained several large streets all very like one another, and many small streets still more like one another, inhabited by people equally like one another, who all went in and out at the same hours, with the same sound upon the same pavements, to do the same work, and to whom every day was the same as yesterday and tomorrow, and every year the counterpart of the last and the next.

These attributes of Coketown were in the main inseparable from the work by which it was sustained; against them were to be set off, comforts of life which found their way all over the world, and elegancies of life which made, we will not ask how much of the fine lady, who could scarcely bear to hear the place mentioned. The rest of its features were voluntary, and they were these.

You saw nothing in Coketown but what was severely workful. If the members of a religious persuasion built a chapel there—as the members of eighteen religious persuasions had done—they made it a pious warehouse of red brick, with sometimes (but this is only in highly ornamental examples) a bell in a birdcage on the top of it. The solitary exception was the New Church; a stuccoed edifice with a square steeple over the door, terminating in four short pinnacles like florid wooden legs. All the public inscriptions in the town were painted alike, in severe characters of black and white. The jail might have been the infirmary, the infirmary might have been the jail, the town-hall might have been either, or both, or anything else, for anything that appeared to the contrary in the graces of their construction. Fact, fact, fact, everywhere in the material aspect of the town; fact, fact, fact, everywhere in the immaterial. The M'Choakum-child school was all fact, and the school of

design was all fact, and the relations between master and man were all fact, and
everything was fact between the lying-in hospital and the cemetery, and what you
couldn't state in figures, or show to be purchaseable in the cheapest market and
saleable in the dearest, was not, and never should be, world without end, Amen.

A Dominant Reading

A dominant reading of this passage sees it as a powerfully realistic description and
condemnation of industrialization. In this view, Dickens has described a grimy
Victorian town in order to reveal the activities of industry as inhuman and unnatural.

In Pairs

List all of the references and phrases which could be used to demonstrate that the
passage is an attack on industrialization. Then consider which of the following
arguments such a reading might "find in" the passage: Industrialization is bad
because it

- pollutes the environment;
- makes life too easy for people;
- isn't "natural";
- dehumanizes people by making them more like machines;
- concentrates wealth in the hands of a few people;
- uses up resources recklessly;
- replaces variety with sameness;
- replaces moral and spiritual motives with profit motives.

Ambiguities in the Text

Like all readings, however, this dominant reading is selective about what counts as
evidence in the passage; it ignores silences which contradict it; and, like most
readings, it doesn't acknowledge the possibility of other readings or interpretations
of the passage.

The following is a summary of a range of other possible readings of the extract.
In pairs, find sentences or phrases in the passage that might be used to support each
of the following readings: The passage

- condemns the working class for not having the strength of character to change
  their circumstances;
- sympathizes with the working classes, who are shackled and oppressed throughout their lives;
- condemns the wealthy for living off the labor of the poor;
- suggests that, nevertheless, some good comes from the unpleasantness of life in
  the town.

The fact that readers *can* find evidence for each of these sometimes contradictory readings suggests that the passage is not a unified and coherent whole. Rather, it can be considered a collection of fragments, which readers unify according to a particular reading practice that fills gaps and makes meanings in the light of a particular set of ideas about the world.

Silences in the Text

In the dominant reading, one of the criticisms made in the passage is that the things produced in Coketown do not reveal the environment in which they were manufactured. The fine ladies who use the products can "scarcely bear to hear the place mentioned." This might suggest that industrialization involves deception—a separation of the product from its means of production.

Dickens wrote *Hard Times* as a serial, with episodes being published in a newspaper. Which of the following descriptions from the passage might also be considered applicable to the newspaper publishing industry?

- "a river that ran purple with ill smelling dye"
- "severe characters of black and white"
- "people . . . who went in at the same hours . . . to do the same work, and to whom every day was the same as yesterday"
- "machinery and tall chimneys"
- "serpents of smoke"

Is it possible that this piece of writing, like the industrial activity it criticizes, remains silent about its own industrial origins? Does the dominant reading contribute to "silence" on any other issues? For example, how might the reference "painted face of a savage" now be read?

Whose Reality?

Recent literary theory argues that texts do *not* simply describe or reflect a given reality. To the contrary, it is argued that texts attempt to construct "reality" in particular terms and to promote particular versions of it for particular purposes on behalf of particular groups of people. How does this challenge the view that Dickens's novel is

- a realistic description of a Victorian industrial town?
- a true and accurate reflection of the times he lived in?
- an accurate picture of the evils of industrialization?

In Groups

Readers have become so good at using one set of reading practices that it has come to seem "natural" to read in this way. The following student, for example, has been trained to use a dominant reading practice. As you read her commentary on the passage, decide which of the following assumptions seem to be a part of her reading practice.

1. Literature offers reflections of the real world.

2. The "meaning" of a text is determined by reading practices.

3. Literary texts are complete structures.

4. There is a meaning hidden or contained in the text.

5. Meanings in the text were put there by the author.

6. Texts have potential meanings rather than actual meanings.

7. The reader's job is to remake the author's meaning.

> This is a very realistic description of the kind of town which sprang up in England following the industrial revolution. Dickens makes the description come to life by giving the reader plenty of details about the town. He portrays the buildings, the machines, and the people, commenting on the noise and dirt to be found there. He uses metaphors ("interminable serpents of smoke") and similes ("like the head of an elephant") to help the reader understand what the scene was like. In his writing style Dickens mocks the factory-like qualities of the town, where everything repeats over and over, and where mass produced goods are created. He repeats "fact, fact, fact" to emphasize the repetitious activity, and he uses long, repetitive sentences to reproduce the feeling of never ending conveyor-belts of items.

> It is a successful piece of writing because it shows how degrading life in such a town was. The people have no comforts; even their churches are like factories, so there is no rest from work. As a writer, Dickens was appalled at the mechanization, a place where there are no arts or recreations, only slavery to the machines of mass production.

Same Practice, Different Reading

Using the same reading practice does not mean, however, that readers will produce or construct identical readings. Here is a response that might have been written by another reader—a factory owner from the nineteenth century. This reader also uses the dominant reading practice and assumes that, as he reads, he is simply finding the meaning in the passage (put there by Mr. Dickens), but his conclusions are quite different from the student's. He fills gaps and make inferences, using ways of thinking available in his culture, which support very different values.

> Mr. Dickens has once again shown us what a keen observer he is, for his description of Coketown is in every sense an expression of my own perception. Here we have a writer who understands the difficulty of working with a class of people who have neither the wit nor the determination to make anything of themselves in this life, and whose contribution to industry is characterised by idleness and foolishness. Mr. Dickens is

right to invoke the image of savages with paint on their faces, an image which aptly describes my employees, who exhibit neither intelligence nor the ability to maintain common standards of cleanliness. Their sullen expressions and constant ill-humour indeed make the factory towns places of "melancholy madness." Small wonder it is that ladies of refinement cannot bear to hear mention of these places, for the mere word conjures images of people who behave like animals, blindly stumbling to and from their work without ever trying to improve themselves, just as they blindly stumble from lying-in hospital to cemetery. If England is ever to reap the benefits of mechanisation, it will be in spite of her working classes, and no thanks to them. We need more people like Mr. Dickens, who might hold up a mirror to the masses and show them the error of their ways.

- ■ How does this reading differ from that of the student above?
- ■ How would you choose between the two readings? Which reading would you support? Why? Would your decision be based on the "accuracy" or "truth" of the reading, or on some other grounds, such as moral values?

These examples are reminders that every reading works to support the values of particular groups of people—factory owners, workers, teachers, students, and so on. There is no such thing as a "natural" or "objective" reading. It is important that account is taken of the values supported by texts and readings when we evaluate them, for the whole practice of producing texts and readings of them is bound up with the way power is structured in society. We must ask, Whose way of life is supported by this reading? Whose interests does it serve? At whose expense is it made?

Readings and Rereadings: "Phone Call"

Following is a short story which has generated or produced a variety of readings from different readers. Read the story, "Phone Call" by Berton Roueche, and then complete the activities which follow it.

Phone Call _____

Berton Roueche

I got out of the truck and got down on my knees and twisted my neck and looked underneath. Everything looked O.K. There wasn't anything hanging down or anything. I got up and opened the hood and looked at the engine. I don't know too much about engines—only what I picked up working around Lindy's Service Station the summer before last. But the engine looked O.K., too. I slammed down the hood and lighted a cigarette. It really had me beat. A school bus from that convent over in Sag Harbour came piling around the bend, and all the girls leaned out the windows and yelled. I just waved. They didn't mean anything by it—just a bunch of kids going home. The bus went on up the road and into the woods and out of sight. I got back in the truck and started it up again. It sounded fine. I put it in gear and let out the clutch and gave it the gas, and nothing happened. The bastard just sat there. So it was probably the transmission. I shut it off and got out. There was nothing to do but call the store. I still had three or four deliveries that had to be made and it was getting kind of late. I knew what Mr. Lester would say, but this was one time when he couldn't blame me. It wasn't my fault. It was him himself that told me to take the truck.

There was a house just up the road—a big white house at the edge of the woods, with a white Rambler station wagon standing in the drive. I dropped my cigarette in a pot-hole puddle and started up the road, and stopped. A dog was laying there in the grass beside the station wagon. It put up its head and—oh, Jesus! It was one of those German police dogs. I turned around and headed the other way. There was another house back there around the bend. I remembered passing it. I went by the truck and walked down the road and around the bend, and the house was there. It was a brown shingle house with red shutters, and there was a sign in one of the windows: "Piano Lessons." The name on the mail box was Timothy. I couldn't tell if there was anybody home or not. There wasn't any car around, but there was a garage at the end of the drive, and it could be parked in there. I went up the drive and around to the kitchen door, and when I got close I could hear a radio talking and laughing inside. I knocked on the door.

The radio went off. Then the door opened a crack and a woman looked out. She had bright blonde hair and little eyes and she was forty years old at least. "Yes?" she said.

"Mrs. Timothy?" I said. "I work for the market over in Bridgehampton, Mrs. Timothy, and my truck—"

"How do you know my name?" she said.

"What?" I said. "Why—it's on the mailbox. I just read it on the mailbox."

"Oh," she said. She licked her lips. "And you say you work for a market?"

"That's right," I said. "The market over in Bridgehampton. And my truck's broke down. So I wondered—"

"What market?" she said.

"Why, Lester's Market," I said. "You know—over in Bridgehampton?"

"I see," she said.

"That's right," I said. "And my truck's broke down. I wondered could I use your phone to call the store and tell them?"

"Well," she said. She looked at me for about a minute. Then she stepped back and opened the door. She had on a pink sweater and one of those big, wide skirts with big, wide pockets and she was nothing but skin and bones. "The telephone's in the living room. I'll show you."

I followed her through the kitchen and across the hall into the living room. I guess that was where she gave her music lessons, too. There was a piano there against the wall and a music stand and a couple of folding chairs, and on top of the piano was a clarinet and one of those metronomes and a big pile of sheet music. The telephone was on a desk between the windows.

"I don't suppose you need the book?" Mrs. Timothy said.

"What?" I said.

"The telephone book," she said. "You know the number of your store, I hope?"

"Oh sure," I said.

"Very well," she said. She reached up and straightened the "Piano Lessons" sign in the window. "Then go ahead and make your—"

She turned around, and she had the funniest look on her face. I mean, it was real strange. It was like she was scared or something.

"I thought you said you had a truck?" she said. "I don't see any truck out there."

"My truck?" I said. "Oh, it's up around the bend. That's where it broke down. You can't see it from here."

"I see," she said, and looked at me. She still had that funny look on her face. Even her voice sounded funny. "I'm here alone, but I want you to know something," she said. "I don't live alone. I'm married. I've got a husband, and he'll be home any minute. He gets off work early today."

She came away from the window. "So my advice to you is to make your call just as quickly as you can."

"O.K.," I said, but I didn't get it. I watched her go across the room and through the hall to the kitchen. I didn't get it at all. She acted almost like I'd done something. I heard a car on the road and looked out. I thought maybe it might be her husband, but it was some guys in a beat-up '59 Impala. But so what if it was her husband? I mean, Jesus—she really had me going. I turned back to the desk and picked up the phone. A woman's voice said, "But, of course, I never let on. I simply—"

I put down the phone and lighted a cigarette, and wandered down the room. I stopped at the piano and looked at the pile of sheet music. There was none of them songs I ever heard of. I looked around for an ashtray, and I found a big white clamshell. It looked like they used it for that. It was on a little table next to an easy chair. Then I went back and tried the phone again. The woman was still talking. I listened for a moment, but it sounded like she was still going strong. I was beginning to get kind of worried. I looked at my watch. It was almost four o'clock . I went over to the clamshell and punched out my cigarette, but I guess I was in too big a hurry. I punched too hard or something, and the clamshell flipped off the table. I made a grab, but I only touched it, and it skidded across the rug. I squatted down and picked it up, and, thank God, it wasn't broken. I must have broke its fall. It wasn't even cracked.

I heard Mrs. Timothy coming. The cigarette butt had rolled under the chair, and I brushed the ashes after it. Mrs. Timothy came through the door, and stopped. Her mouth fell open.

"It's O.K.," I said. "It didn't even—"

"What were you doing in that table drawer?" she said.

"What?" I said.

"I said what were you doing in that table drawer?" she said.

I shook my head. "Nothing," I said. "What drawer? I mean, I wasn't doing anything in any drawer. I just accidentally dropped this ashtray. I dropped it and I was just picking it up."

Mrs. Timothy didn't say anything. She just stood there and looked at me. Then she cleared her throat. "Well," she said. "Did you make your call?"

"Not yet," I said. "The line was busy."

"Oh?" she said. "And how do you know that? I didn't hear you dial or even say a word."

"I don't mean the store," I said. "I mean the party line. It was your line was busy."

She gave me one of those looks. Something sure was eating her. She walked over to the desk and picked up the phone and listened. Then she held it out. I could hear the buzz of the empty line. She put down the phone. "I suppose they just this minute hung up," she said. "Is that what I'm supposed to believe?"

"There was somebody talking before," I said. "I tried twice."

"I don't know what you have in mind, but I advise you to forget it," she said. "I'm not easily fooled. I'm really not as stupid as you seem to think. I know what's going on these days. I read the papers, you know. I hear the news, and I've heard about boys like you. I know all about them. I didn't want to let you in. I only did it against my better judgment. I had a feeling about you the minute I opened the door." She stood back against the desk. "I don't believe you had a breakdown. I don't believe it for a minute. If you broke down where you say you did, you were practically in front of Miller's, so that's where you would have gone to phone. You wouldn't have come all the way down here. I don't think you even *have* a truck. I think you came through the woods." She took a deep breath. "And now I want you to leave. I want you to get out of my house."

"I don't know what you're talking about, Mrs. Timothy," I said. "I just want to call the store. I've *got* to call the store."

"I said get out of my house," she said.

"O.K.," I said. "O.K., but—"

"I said get out," she said. She reached in one of the pockets of her big skirt and brought out a knife. It was a kitchen knife, with a long blade honed down thin. She pointed it at me like a gun.

"Hey!" I said.

"Oh, I see," she said. "That changes things. It's a different story now, isn't it? You didn't know I could take care of myself, did you?" She came away from the desk. "You thought I was just another helpless woman, didn't you?"

I stepped back a couple of steps.

"Hey," I said. "For God's sake, what do you—"

"What's the matter?" she said. "You're not afraid of me are you?" She moved the knife. "A big, strong, tough boy like you?"

I stepped back again.

"You *are* a big, strong, tough boy," she said. "Aren't you?"

"For God's sake Mrs. Timothy," I said. "I don't know what you're talking about. I wasn't doing anything."

She kind of smiled. "A great, big, strong, tough boy," she said.

I didn't say anything. The way she was looking at me, I couldn't hardly think, I couldn't hardly believe it. It was like it was all a dream. I took another step, stumbled into one of the folding chairs. Then I was up against the piano. I looked at the knife coming at me and my heart began to jump. She meant it. She really meant it, but that didn't mean I had to just stand there and let her. I slid along the front of the piano and reached up and touched the metronome and pushed it away and stretched and found the clarinet and grabbed it.

She let out a kind of yell. "Don't you dare!" she said. "You put that down!" She raised the knife. "Put that clarinet down."

But I had a good grip on it now. I looked at the knife with the point coming at me, and swung. I swung at it hard as I could. I felt it connect, it tingled all the way up my arm. The knife went sailing across the room and I heard it hit the wall. Mrs. Timothy didn't move. She just stood there, and she was holding her wrist. It wasn't bleeding or anything, but it looked kind of funny and loose. Then she began to scream.

On Your Own

Take a few moments to write down your thoughts about the story, responding to the following questions:

■ Without just retelling the story, explain the reading you have constructed.
■ Try to describe how you constructed your reading. What reading practice did you use? To help you with this question, here is a list of techniques and approaches you might have applied. Did you

—assume that the story has a meaning which could be uncovered?
—look for some kind of general message about life and people?
—ask yourself what the author had in mind?

—imagine the characters as real people?
—look for an explanation which made sense of every detail in the story?
—measure the story against your own real-life experiences?
—consider how point of view and writing style influenced your reading of the story?

Or are you unsure about how you arrived at your reading? Why? When you have finished making your notes, compare your response to the story with that of other group members. Do you all agree on the "meaning"?

Readings

Included below are four widely varying commentaries about "Phone Call." Read the statements carefully, looking for points of agreement and disagreement between them.

Commentary 1

What Roueche offers us in this story is an unambiguous portrait of the alienation which pervades contemporary society. He captures realistically the simple inability of people to communicate with each other.

The tension in the story comes from the reader's desire for the two characters to "engage" with each other, to see beyond their own situations and recognize how things look to another human being. Roueche guarantees this tension through his choice of characters. The young truck driver is naively innocent of the effect his actions are having on the woman. The woman, for her part, is living in a self-contained world of hysterical fear which prevents her from seeing things as they really are. . . .

Commentary 2

The richness of this story is due to its basic ambiguity. While the story line and meaning are clear enough on one level, there are many clues which suggest otherwise. There are undercurrents of entrapment in this story, suggestions that the woman is not as innocent as she seems. She is like a spider waiting in its web for the unsuspecting fly. On this occasion the victim is a young man whose truck has broken down. He comes to the house for help. The woman's outward behavior toward the man suggests that she is uncomfortable about having strangers in the house. Yet she has a sign in the window advertising herself as a piano teacher, so she must have many comparative strangers come to her home. This is an inconsistency which draws attention to itself, for the woman adjusts the sign in the window once the man is inside. Is she really so fearful, or is it an act? The sign seems symbolically to advertise her civility, yet it conflicts with her behavior.

Her questioning of the stranger is similarly ambiguous. While she might be trying to establish the accuracy of his story—for her own peace of mind—she might also be calculating the likelihood of anyone tracing him to her home. She establishes that no one would expect him to have come to her house, for his truck is nowhere in sight and there are other houses around the bend, nearer to where he says he broke down. Most interesting of all is the woman's change in behavior once she has the knife. Her repetition of the phrase "big, strong, tough boy" suggests a kind of sexual advance on her part, though her intentions are clearly more violent. There is something predatory in her actions. . . .

It is not enough to read this story as a misunderstanding between a confused young man and a frightened woman. Such a reading does not explain the woman's sudden shift of character. Yet there isn't enough information for the reader to confirm the suspicion that this woman is a murderess in the Hitchcock tradition. It is this very ambiguity which makes the story so fascinating, since it reflects the confusion and incoherence of modern life.

Commentary 3
A nasty little story, "Phone Call" pretends to portray the wide-eyed surprise that men experience whenever they try to understand women. An unbelievably innocent young man relates his confusion at finding himself trapped in a house by a hysterical housewife who thinks he has plans to take advantage of her. Neither of the characters is convincing. He is too, too naive. I can just hear him telling this one to the boys at the pub: "Women—I'll never understand them". She is the stereotyped hysteric: sexually frustrated ("You are a big, strong, tough boy"), paranoid, trapped in her domesticity.

It stops just short of condoning wife beating on the grounds that women must be controlled. I would have stabbed him, too.

Commentary 4
Roueche's "Phone Call" permits the reader to observe the "logic" of male domination in action. The two characters are superficially cast in stereotypical roles: the man is strong, rational, mobile. He drives a truck. The woman is frail, fearful, and housebound. She gives music lessons. But these stereotyped characterizations are undercut throughout the story, resulting in an ironic reversal of positions.

The narrative—which is given from the male's point of view—reveals a kind of bovine stupidity in the young truck driver. It is hardly credible that he should find the woman's actions so mystifying. Furthermore, his fear of the German shepherd dog, his lack of knowledge about the truck he drives, and his discomfort in the woman's presence all contrive to subvert the male stereotype. By contrast, the woman is quick witted and perceptive. She sees immediately the inconsistencies in his story, and she makes it clear to him that she is not about to be fooled. When he lingers suspiciously, she prepares to defend herself. The narrative tries to conceal all of this by coloring the portrait of the woman. He thinks she is strange. He presents her merely as a body—"she was nothing but skin and bones." But this is a man, speaking to men, and his perception of the woman must be challenged. It is he who is at fault. His arrogant assumption that his innocence is "obvious" is what causes the eventual conflict.

What is obscured by the language of the narrative is the male's surprise at finding a complete human being where he expected a mere shell. The woman in the story exhibits many of the qualities for which men are traditionally praised: resourcefulness, perception, a willingness to act. It is surely this which our narrator finds "strange," and at the end of the story he resorts to using physical strength to punish the woman for her masculine behavior. But his action is defensive; hers is aggressive. The roles have been reversed.

On Your Own

Using the following format, make notes about the reading each commentary has constructed of various aspects of the story. The final section of the chart, concerning "the relationship between literature and life," covers a complex area. You might consider which of the following seems to sum up the commenter's view: (a) literary texts simply reflect life; (b) literary texts comment on life; (c) literary texts have nothing to do with life; (d) literary texts show what life should be like; (e) literary texts express the author's view of life.

1. The woman and her actions
Commenter 1
Commenter 2
Commenter 3
Commenter 4
2. The man and his actions
Commenter 1
Commenter 2
Commenter 3
Commenter 4
3. The message or theme of the story
Commenter 1
Commenter 2
Commenter 3
Commenter 4
4. The relationship between literature and life
Commenter 1
Commenter 2
Commenter 3
Commenter 4

Compare your notes with a partner's and discuss any differences in your readings of each commenter's position.

The puzzling thing is that each of the commenters' responses can seem quite plausible in itself, but many of the readings contradict each other. This conflicts with the idea that "practical criticism" is about finding the "true meaning" of the text.

If it is not possible to assert the "true meaning" of a text, then perhaps instead of asking which is the correct reading, it might be more productive to ask how each of these readings is constructed and for what purposes. Who or what, for example, is supported by each of these readings?

Constructing Readings

One way of analyzing the construction of each of these readings is to see them as the result of the commenters doing the following as they read:

- emphasizing particular aspects or "textual features" of the text;
- ignoring or suppressing particular aspects or "textual features";
- reading selected "textual features" to "fit" an interpretation;
- filling gaps with ideas, available in their culture, which support particular ways of thinking and acting.

A Better Model of Literary Production

At the beginning of this chapter you saw a simple model of the traditional explanation of literary production. The diagram in Figure 1 gives a more modern explanation. It shows how social structures determine the meanings which writers and readers make with literary texts.

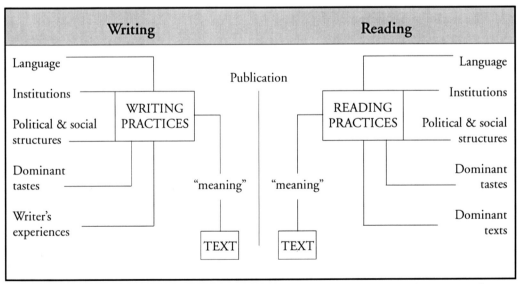

Figure 1: Modern explanation of literary production

In this model there is no one-way transmission of ideas from author to reader. Instead, cultural factors shape the kind of writing and reading which can be done, thereby applying meaning to the text. The author's experiences are only one of a (much more powerful) range of influences on how a text is made. In this model, "literary" texts and their meanings are a result of cultural production.

In Groups

Compare this model with the diagram your group produced at the start of this chapter.

■ What important differences are there between the two models?
■ Which aspects of your original model do you still support? Which would you change? Why?

"School"

Peter Cowan's story "School" has been included in many anthologies and collections. Read it, and then work through the activities that follow. These provide a suggested outline for studying any literary text.

School

Peter Cowan

The classroom was hot, and outside the sun was hard on the dusty earth and the grass was going brown on the playing fields. The boy looked at his exercise book, at the figures and the red-pencil corrections, and they were nothing, related to nothing in his experience. He raised his eyes very slowly and saw the hard light and the bare ground and the dying grass. Over the fence the two old jarrahs with the spread tops framed the piled houses of the suburbs. He had his hands to his head and he looked out of the low window and then back at the figures on the paper, and slowly the tears began to force their way on him. He made no sound and the others working did not know.

Now out beyond him were the wide flat acres of wheat, heavy in ear, and the cut patches bare to earth dotted with the stooks. The wagon moved slowly out, and when they reached the stooks his father began to pitch hay. The sheaves thumped on the wagon. He helped Ted, who worked for them, to build the load. As the wagon started for the next stook he felt the jolt and looked at the load to see if it would hold. High up he sat when it was built and they drove in to the stack. He got on the stack and Ted threw the sheaves to him and he passed to his father. The sun was hard on the paddocks and the dull scrub and the few trees. It made the wagon hot and the hay held the heat, and his clothes were hot. It was hard to say when the shadows first started to come on the ground, but they began to shift out from the stooks and from the stack and about the few shade-trees. When they were tired with the mid-afternoon he saw his mother coming out with the tea. They sat in the shade of the wagon and he listened to the talk and he knew the people and the wheat and the town and the bulk bin and when he said something they listened and answered. The colours began to change slowly, to deepen, and shift from the smooth acres of the wheat and the fallow and old stubble, and from the dulling scrub that was making a dark edge about the paddock. The sun went from the hot ground and they left the wagon outside the stack and took the horses out. Ted led them to the yard, while he put out the feeds. In the quiet darkening stables, after Ted and his father had gone, he watched the heads in the boxes and listened to the noises the horses made, together, feeding. When the stables and the shed with the bags of stored wheat became dark he pushed open the iron door and went across the yard. There was the light in the house and they sat at the meal and there was talk and if he wanted to say something they listened.

He could feel the tears and he was afraid to move lest the others see. He looked at the symbols on the paper and they blurred and made no pattern. His hands sheltered his face, and he looked slowly up and to one side and he saw the blackboard and the desks and shelves and the maps that were pinned to the walls.

Analyzing the Construction of Readings

The following activities will lead you through stages which should prove useful for examining any literary text. They begin by focusing on a distinction between "what is on the page" and what readers make of this. This is not a straightforward distinction because readers do seem to find different things "on the page." Although texts seem to be complete and to offer very full descriptions and accounts, frequently this is because of reading practices which encourage the unconscious filling of gaps so that readers are unaware of them and their filling of them. Looking closely at "what is on the page"—the "text information"—can be, however, a useful starting point from which to analyze the construction of different readings of a text.

What Is "On the Page"?

On your own, summarize the text of "School" by completing the following list of statements. List only what is stated.

Paragraph 1
- The classroom is hot.
- A boy is in a schoolroom.
- He looks out through the window.
- He looks at figures on the paper.
- He starts to cry.

Paragraph 2
•
•
•
•

Paragraph 3
•
•
•
•

When you have completed your summary, share your list with a partner. Exclude statements based on assumptions. For example: "The boy is crying because he doesn't like school." The text does *not* state this. The reason for his crying is inferred or produced by the reader from the range of meanings or ways of thinking about such an occurrence (that is, a boy crying) available in her or his culture.

Text Information

Discuss, in pairs, whether each of the following statements is provable on the basis of text information alone, or whether it is constructed by filling gaps. The first item has been done for you.

Statement	Construction
1. The middle paragraph is a reminiscence. It describes what the boy is thinking about while in the classroom.	This is a reader's assumption. The paragraphs may detail three quite separate incidents. There is nothing in the story to indicate how the three paragraphs relate to each other.
2. The boy is crying because school cuts him off from the world he knows.	
3. The classroom is sterile and unfriendly.	
4. The boy is lonely at school.	
5. The boy prefers farm life to school life.	

Which statements below might be challenged using text information? Quote sections of the text which could be used to challenge each point.

Statement	Challenge
1. The boy does not live on a farm. He is a city dweller whose family once holidayed on a relative's farm.	
2. The boy enjoys school but is upset at getting a math problem wrong.	
3. The boy has many good friends at school.	
4. The boy is unhappy because he enjoys neither school nor life on the farm, where the work is hard and hot and people pay attention to him only when he speaks up and reminds them that he is there.	

In Groups

Share your findings from the previous activities; then discuss each of the following points.

■ Look carefully at any "evidence" which group members supply. Are their conclusions based on text information, or have they drawn conclusions based on their reading assumptions?
■ How have these activities affected your reading of the text so far? Does its "meaning" now seem more or less obvious? Why is this?

On Your Own: Writing

Choose three of the statements below about "School." Write a paragraph to support each, using argument and quotations to develop your reading.

■ "School" contrasts the sterile, artificial experience of school with the pleasing harmony of a life close to nature.
■ "School" demonstrates that farm life is no more natural than any other existence—it has its own cultural practices, both social and technological.

- "School" condemns the rigidity and competitiveness of modern education.
- "School" implicitly supports the repression of women in rural communities.
- "School" offers a falsely romantic view of rural life and an unfairly critical view of city life.
- "School" derives its main effect from the use of setting.
- "School" derives its main effect from the use of structure.

When you have finished writing, ask class members to read samples of their work so that all statements are represented. As a class, discuss:

- the conflicting readings which emerge;
- groups of people who might support particular readings;
- which readings individual class members support, and why.

In Pairs

Look back over the work you have done on "School." Make a list of the steps you worked through in analyzing the text and how it might be read. Note what you did at each stage, and some of the questions you asked. Keep this list in your file and use it as a guide when you are faced with similar tasks in the future.

Writing about Reading "School"

1. You have now spent considerable time writing, talking, and thinking about "School." Use this work as the basis for a piece of writing titled "Reading 'School.'" Use headings if you wish, and discuss the following areas in your writing:

- the text information that readers have to work with;
- how reading practices and reader assumptions make meanings from text information;
- gaps, silences, or contradictions that are apparent in your reading of the text;
- the range of readings that can be constructed from the text and the ideas and values that might be supported by each.

Support your discussion with references to the text and examples from your activities and discussions.

2. Rewrite "School" from the point of view of the boy himself, using a first person narrator. Keep to the three-paragraph structure, and make only those changes which are necessary to support the shift in point of view. When you have finished, discuss how the point of view alters:

- the text information presented to readers;
- the way in which readers might construct meaning from the text.

3. This chapter has focused on how modern theories of literature account for the meanings of literary texts. There has been a shift away from the idea that meaning exists in the text, and a shift toward the idea that meaning is constructed through the reading of the text. Discuss this new way of thinking about literary meaning. Support your essay with references to:

■ the work you have done in this chapter;
■ your experiences as a reader and a writer;
■ your previous schooling.

When you have finished, share the writing and discuss the issues that have been raised.

Reading in Terms of Gender

■ What is gender and how is it constructed?
■ What part does "literature" play in the power structures of society?
■ Do all representations of gender reinforce cultural prejudices and stereotypes?
■ How can readers challenge representations of gender in literary texts?

Literature and Power

Cultural concepts of literature are closely tied to wider beliefs and values. Because of this, literary traditions and social structures tend to give each other mutual support. The ideas of dominant groups tend to be emphasized or foregrounded in literary activities, while those of less powerful groups tend to be suppressed. In modern terms, the values and beliefs of less powerful groups are said to be "silenced" or marginalized. In this chapter, you will examine literary texts from the perspective of one group which is often marginalized: women.

Power and Gender

In many western cultures, the largest dominant group of all consists of men. Historically, power has rested with men and been handed on to men. A society in which power is distributed in this way is called a patriarchy.

One strategy by which the patriarchal system is maintained is that it constructs gender for people. While "sex" is a biological matter, "gender" is a cultural one.

Naturalizing Gender

Patriarchal cultures do not admit that gender is constructed for people. Instead, they try to blur the distinction between biology and culture by making gender roles seem natural. The process of naturalizing gender takes place not only through social structures but also through language and literary texts. In groups, discuss the use of the word "man" in each of these sentences:

"That's one small step for a man, one giant leap for mankind" (Neil Armstrong, stepping onto the moon). "We hold these truths to be self-evident, that all men are created equal . . ." (U.S. Constitution). "What a piece of work is a man!" (*Hamlet* II.ii)

■ What is the effect of recording human history and thought in terms of male achievement? To what extent are the achievements and activities of women silenced or marginalized by this technique?

■ How do you respond to arguments that the term "man" naturally includes "woman"? Is this a natural arrangement, or is it culturally constructed?

On your own, record the "dictionary" meanings and the connotations or associations of these words:

man	woman
master	mistress
husband	wife
gentleman	lady

With a partner, discuss these pairs of words:

husband—master	wife—mistress
man—gentleman	woman—lady

■ How do the connotations of "master" and "mistress" and of "gentleman" and "lady" differ?

■ What gender messages are conveyed by the differences?

Discuss the meanings of the words below. Are there female equivalents?

Term	Meanings	Equivalents
Man (verb)		
Man (noun)		
Husbandry		
Manpower		
Mastery		

In groups, share and discuss the results of these activities. They demonstrate an important point about the links between language, power, and the way people see the world. The words we use do not simply label ideas and objects that already exist; they construct particular versions of the world.

The Language of Patriarchy

As well as naturalizing gender through language and social organizations, patriarchal cultures try to hide or obscure differences which exist in society. Rather than acknowledge the diversity of races, beliefs, and classes, they strive to give the impression that society is homogeneous—composed of people who all look, act, and think the same. This has the effect of silencing or marginalizing particular groups.

This Is Australia?

The following passage is taken from Ian Moffitt's essay "Leisure" in *This Is Australia*, a book about Australian culture. Like most populations, Australians are a diverse people. How much of this diversity is reflected in the passage?

> The pursuit of leisure is a serious business in Australia. Those of us who couldn't care less about racing (and there are a lot) dig gardens, paint bedrooms, go to the local flicks, do a hundred-and-one other things. But, en masse, we're leisure lovers: a healthy, but not fit, people with a premature paunch as a symbol of our mindless affluence.

> Take the surf. The old Australia was a bronzed lifesaver stamping into the future with a flag unfurling above him and a big yellow A on the front of his green costume. He was a young nation marching nobly out of War and Depression, with Right and Manhood still unquestioned, Patriotism unchallenged, Service and Sacrifice realistic ideals.

> We were (we imagined) kings of the creaming-lemonade water, idols of the world, and the lifesaver in peace became the Digger in war, the myth-men melting into each other.

Individually, list words and phrases in the passage which have the effect of silencing or obscuring the roles of women in Australia. Then comment on the following aspects of the passage. Discuss your findings in small groups.

1. The use of the first-person plural, "we." Who does "we" refer to? What does it try to suggest about the relationship between narrator and reader?

2. The passage makes reference to a number of cultural myths by discussing "lifesavers" and "Diggers." Does Australian culture have any such myths about women? If so, how do they differ from the male myths? If not, why not?

3. What other differences are obscured by the passage? (What, for example, does it suggest about race, social class, and age in Australian society?)

Challenging Patriarchy

One way to challenge the patriarchy of literary texts is to read them from the perspective of "silenced" groups. In this way, previously obscured elements can be emphasized or foregrounded. Read these two poems by Robert Frost (1875–1963) and, in pairs, work through the activities which follow each one.

Never Again Would Birds' Song Be the Same

Robert Frost

He would declare and could himself believe
That the birds there in all the garden round
From having heard the daylong voice of Eve
Had added to their own an oversound,
Her tone of meaning but without the words.
Admittedly an eloquence so soft
Could only have had an influence on birds
When call or laughter carried it aloft.
Be that as may be, she was in their song.
Moreover her voice upon their voices crossed
Had now persisted in the woods so long
That probably it never would be lost.
Never again would birds' song be the same,
And to do that to birds was why she came.

This poem can be read as a fable or legend about the coming of Eve and the influence she had on "nature," represented by the song of the birds. What answers might this dominant reading provide to the following questions?

1. What does Eve contribute to the natural world?

2. Is her contribution accidental or intentional?

3. What image of "woman" is constructed by this reading? For example: active or passive? intellectual or emotional? part of nature or part of culture?

4. Does this reading construct Eve as (a) an integral part of nature? (b) a superior civilizing influence? or (c) an inferior, disrupting influence?

5. Who is the "He" referred to in the poem? Why is this masculine element introduced?

The Aim Was Song

Robert Frost

Before man came to blow it right
The wind once blew itself untaught,

And did its loudest day and night
In any rough place where it caught.
Man came to tell it what was wrong:
It hadn't found the place to blow;
It blew too hard—the aim was song.
And listen—how it ought to go.
He took a little in his mouth,
And held it long enough for north
To be converted into south,
And then by measure blew it forth.
By measure. It was word and note,
The wind the wind had meant to be—
A little through the lips and throat.
The aim was song—the wind could see.

The second poem, "The Aim Was Song," can be read as constructing a similar scenario to "Never Again Would Birds' Song Be the Same." However, it focuses on the influence of man, not woman. Write brief answers to the following questions.

1. What does man appear to contribute to the natural world?

2. Is his contribution accidental or intentional?

3. Is "Man" presented as (a) an integral part of nature? (b) a superior civilizing influence? or (c) an inferior, disrupting influence?

4. What image of man is constructed by the poem?

5. Why does this poem use the general term "man" rather than a specific individual —for example, "Adam"?

Summarize your readings by completing this comparison table. Under each heading, list the attributes that might be given to the man and woman in these dominant readings.

Man	Woman
1. Actively instructs nature.	2. Is passively overhead (the wind) by nature (the birds).

In Groups

The table you have completed summarizes some features of dominant readings of these poems. In groups, make a list of points you would challenge or support in these readings. You might begin with the following assumptions:

- that men and women have such different qualities;
- that wind and birdsong stand for "nature";
- that the term "Man" includes "Woman."

Compare your list with those of other groups and then discuss these questions:

1. What beliefs about gender do these readings of the poems support?

2. What specific literary and cultural sources do they appear to draw on? (Are other stories or beliefs pointed to as a basis for the texts?)

3. What groups or ideas are marginalized by the dominant readings you have examined?

Gender and Intertextuality

Gender images are never the product of isolated texts. Any text must be read in terms of its relationship with other texts of the culture. Sometimes a text might make specific references to other works (as in the reference to "Eve" in Frost's poem); at other times the references are less clear. In either case, this interweaving of texts is called intertextuality. Gender images and stereotypes are intertextual. They evolve out of, and, in turn, promote patriarchal ideas and practices.

"A Valediction: Forbidding Mourning" and *The Collector*

Read John Donne's poem "A Valediction: Forbidding Mourning." It was written in 1633, so the language will seem dated. It makes use of an intricate set of comparisons. You may need to read it more than once.

A Valediction: Forbidding Mourning _____

John Donne

As virtuous men pass mildly away,
And whisper to their souls to go,
Whilst some of their sad friends do say
The breath goes now, and some say, no:

So let us melt, and make no noise,
No tear-floods, nor sigh-tempests move,
'Twere profanation of our joys
To tell the laity of our love.

Moving of th' earth brings harms and fears
Men reckon what it did and meant;
But trepidation of the spheres,
Though greater far, is innocent.

Dull sublunary lovers' love
(Whose souls is sense) cannot admit
Absence, because it doth remove
Those things which elemented it.

But we by a love so much refined
That our selves know not what it is,
Inter-assured of the mind,
Care less, eyes, lips, and hands to miss.

Our two souls therefore, which are one,
Though I must go, endure not yet
A breach, but an expansion,
Like gold to airy thinness beat.

If they be two, they are two so
As stiff twin compasses are two;
Thy soul, the fixed foot, makes no show
To move, but doth, if th' other do.

And though it in the centre sit,
Yet when the other far doth roam,
It leans and harkens after it,
And grows erect, as that comes home.

Such wilt though be to me, who must
Like th' other foot, obliquely run;
Thy firmness makes my circle just,
And makes me end where I begun.

A Reading

This brief "explanation" of the poem appears in a textbook on literary studies. It represents a dominant reading of Donne's text. Read the extract; then reread the poem before going on.

"Valediction" proceeds by a series of arresting yet beautifully integrated comparisons. The speaker is addressing his lady on the eve of his departure on a journey. His poem is essentially an argument for a restrained and dignified parting. It might be paraphrased thus: Let us not weep and make a show of our love for everyone to see, for ours is a noble love that is not weakened by physical separation. Our parting should be like the passing away of virtuous men, who take their leave calmly and without protest.

The extract goes on to explain how each of the poem's comparisons builds on the idea that the relationship between the speaker and "lady" is virtuous and refined.

In Groups

Match the following comparisons with stanzas or lines in the poem that could be used to support them.

Comparison or Idea	Stanzas or Lines
Like the two legs of a drawing instrument, the lovers are "joined" at the highest point, so that the stability of one constrains the mobility of the other.	
Gold, because it is pure, can be beaten out to extreme thinness without breaking, whereas less pure valuable metals fracture.	
Earthquakes are violently destructive, but motions of the heavenly bodies are not, for the heavens are free of corruption and evil.	
Partners whose love is purely physical cannot survive a parting because this removes the basis of the relationship.	
This speaker's relationship with his lady is "heavenly" because it is spiritual and rational; purely physical relationships are "earthbound" and therefore corrupt.	

Can you "find" other comparisons in the poem by reading in this way?

Challenging the Reading

Four centuries of critical study have assumed that the speaker of this poem is a male, yet nothing in the poem says it must be so. Part of the reason has to do with a tendency to equate the speaker of a text with its author—in this case, a man. Another reason for the assumption is that the poem supports a series of gender stereotypes when read in this way.

In Pairs

Working from the assumption that the words are spoken by a man to a woman, answer the following questions, backing up your response with quotations or line references.

Question	Answer	Quotation
Which character is mobile?		
Which character is static?		
Which character is emotional?		
Which character is rational?		
Which character is "strong"?		
Which character is "weak"?		
Which character is active?		
Which character is passive?		
Which character speaks?		
Which character listens?		

In what ways do the gender images from this reading correspond to those in readings of the Robert Frost poems? Why might this be? Do these aspects of the poem prevent you from reading it as the speech of a woman? Do they at least make it harder to construct such a reading? How would such a reading—that is, reading it as the speech of a woman to a man—differ from a traditional, patriarchal reading? How might readings of the man's and woman's behavior and motives be changed?

Courtly Love and *The Collector*

The gender stereotypes you have explored recur over and over in readings of western literary texts. For example, Shakespeare's *Romeo and Juliet*, written around 1596, constructs a similar pattern of images. It is Romeo who roams, while Juliet remains in her father's house. She is confined; he is free.

Both Shakespeare and Donne wrote within a literary convention called "courtly love." The convention held that men should be like slaves in their devotion to a woman. It meant putting the woman "on a pedestal" and worshipping her from afar. But putting someone on a pedestal also has the effect of immobilizing that person and of turning her or him into an object to be looked at. To "build your world" around someone might also be to put him or her into a kind of prison.

Here is part of a plot summary of a contemporary novel, *The Collector*, by John Fowles (1926–). Read it and then discuss the questions which follow.

> A solitary young man—Frederick Clegg—develops an obsession for a beautiful young artist named Miranda. Clegg cannot bring himself to speak to Miranda. Instead, he follows and watches her. When he wins a lottery, Clegg purchases a secluded house with a basement. Clegg kidnaps Miranda and locks her in the basement. He hopes that in time she will grow to love him. Once he has Miranda trapped, Clegg learns that she is not the person he imagined her to be. She is a real human being: strong willed, independent, creative. She is all the things he is not. He grows to hate her. Miranda makes numerous escape attempts.

The story continues from here.

Discussion

1. Which of the following features of the courtly love convention are supported by the plot summary of *The Collector*?

   a. The woman is made the center of the man's world.
   b. The woman's role is to be looked at or desired.
   c. The woman's feelings are subordinated to the man.
   d. The woman is confined to a private space; the man is free to stay in the public sphere.
   e. The woman is assumed to be (and therefore expected to be) perfect.
   f. Proper behavior is defined by the man's standards.

2. What ending would you predict for the novel? Why?

3. Suggest other texts which construct gender and relationships in this way. You might draw on examples from television, movies, advertising, and books.

Decentering Woman

Texts make use of conventions for constructing gender. They appear to make women the center or focus of the text. But it could be argued that events in the text are mostly presented from the male point of view. This has the effect of shifting the focus away from the static image of the woman and onto the active image of the man. So, even when the woman seems to be the focus, she is in fact marginalized or decentered.

"Rapunzel"

Read the following story, "Rapunzel," thinking about how the characters are constructed in terms of gender.

- Which character is mobile?
- Which character is "weak"?
- Which character is rational?
- Which character is static?
- Which character is active?
- Which character speaks?
- Which character is emotional?
- Which character is passive?

Rapunzel

Traditional

There was once a man and his wife, and for a long time they had been longing for a child, but in vain. At last, the woman was in hope that heaven would grant her wish. At the back of their house there was a little window overlooking a magnificent garden full of the most beautiful flowers and herbs. However, a high wall surrounded the garden, and no one dared to enter it, for it belonged to a witch who was very powerful and of whom the whole world stood in awe.

One day the woman was standing at this window looking down into the garden, when she noticed a bed which was planted with the finest rampion. It looked so fresh and green that it made her mouth water and she was possessed by the desire to eat some. This craving grew from day to day, but she knew she never could get any. So she began to pine away and looked pale and miserable. Her husband, in great alarm, asked her, "What ails you, my dear?"

"Alas," she replied. "If I can't eat some of the rampion from the garden behind our house, I shall die."

The husband, who loved her, thought, "Rather than let your wife die, you shall fetch her some of the rampion, cost what may." So when dusk came, he climbed over the wall into the witch's garden, hurriedly cut a handful of rampion, and took it to his wife. She at once made it into a salad and ate it up with great lust. She found it so tasty, so very tasty, that her desire grew three times as strong the next day. If it was to be stilled, her husband once more had to climb over into the garden. So at dusk, he let himself down again but just as he had clambered over the wall, his heart stood still, for there was the witch confronting him.

"How dare you come into my garden like a common thief and steal my rampion?" she said eyeing him angrily. "This shall cost you dear."

"Alas," he answered, "temper justice with mercy; it was from dire necessity that I resolved to come. My wife has seen your rampion from her window and her longing is so strong that she will die if she does not get some to eat."

Thereupon the witch's wrath abated, and she said to him, "If it is as you say, I will let you take home as much rampion as you like. Only I make one condition. You must give me the child that your wife is going to give birth to. It will be well off and I will care for it like a mother."

In his anguish the man agreed to everything, and the moment the wife gave birth the witch appeared, christened the child Rapunzel (rampion), and took her away with her.

Rapunzel grew up to be the most beautiful girl under the sun. When she was twelve years old, the witch shut her up in a tower in a forest. It had no stairs or doors, only a little window quite high up at the top. When the witch wanted to get in, she stood down below and called, "Rapunzel, Rapunzel, let down your hair."

Rapunzel had magnificent long hair, as fine as spun gold. When she heard the witch call, she loosened her tresses and wound them round a hook by the window. She let them fall down, and the witch climbed up by Rapunzel's braids.

It came to pass a few years later that the King's son, riding through the forest, came close to the tower. Suddenly, he heard someone singing. The voice was so charming that he stopped to listen. It was Rapunzel who in her loneliness amused herself by letting her sweet voice resound. The Prince wanted to climb up and join her and sought for the tower door but there was none to be found.

He rode home, but the singing had touched his heart so deeply that he went out into the forest every day and listened. Once, as he was standing behind a tree, he saw the witch come near and heard her call, "Rapunzel, Rapunzel, let down your hair."

Then Rapunzel let her braided hair fall down and the witch climbed up.

"If this is the ladder by which to come up," he thought, "I will try my luck once myself."

The very next day, when dusk began to fall, he went up to the tower and cried, "Rapunzel, Rapunzel, let down your hair."

Presently the plaits came down and the King's son climbed up by them. At first, Rapunzel was terribly frightened when a man came into her room, for she had never set eyes on a man in her life. But the Prince talked to her most kindly, telling her that his heart had been so deeply moved by her singing that he knew no peace and had to come and see her. Then Rapunzel lost her fear, and when he asked her if she would take him for her husband, and she saw that he was young and hand-some, she thought, "He will love me better than old Mother Gothel," and she said, "Yes," and laid her hand in his.

She said, "I would be glad to go with you, but I do not know how to get down. Will you bring a skein of silk every time you come? I shall weave it into a ladder, and when it is ready, I will come down, and you will take me on your horse."

They arranged that meanwhile he could always come to see her in the evening, for the old woman came by day. Nor did the witch discover anything until Rapunzel broached her one day and said to her, "Please tell me, Dame Gothel, how is it that you are much heavier to pull up than the young Prince who will be here before long?"

"Oh, you wicked child," yelled the witch, "what do I have to hear from you? I had thought I cut you off from the world, and yet you have deceived me!"

In her rage she clutched Rapunzel's lovely hair, wound it several times round her left hand, picked up a pair of scissors with her right hand, and snip, snap the lovely tresses lay on the ground. She was merciless and took poor Rapunzel into a wilderness, where she was forced to live in greatest wretchedness and sorrow.

Yet on the very day she had cast Rapunzel away, the witch fastened the plaits she had cut off to the window hook. When the Prince came again he cried, "Rapunzel, Rapunzel, let down your hair."

Then the witch lowered the hair. The Prince climbed up, but above he found not his beloved Rapunzel but the witch, who looked at him with evil and venomous eyes.

"Oh ho," she cried mockingly, "you have come to fetch your dearly beloved, but the pretty bird sits no longer in her nest, and she can sing no more, for the cat has snatched her away, and it will scratch your eye out for you, too. Rapunzel is lost to you, you shall never set eyes on her again."

The Prince was beside himself with grief and, in his despair flung himself down from the tower. He escaped with his life, but had his eyes scratched out by thorns among which he fell. He wandered about in the forest blind and feeding on nothing but roots and berries. He could do nothing but lament and weep over the loss of his most beloved Rapunzel. Thus he roamed about in utter misery for some years and, at last, found himself in the wilderness where Rapunzel had been living in dire poverty with the twins that had been born to her, a boy and a girl.

He heard a voice and it seemed to him familiar, so he went on in its direction. When he got there, Rapunzel recognized him and fell on his neck in tears. Two of them wetted his eyes and, at once, his eyes grew quite clear and he could see as well as ever.

He took her and their twins to his kingdom, where he was joyfully received, and they lived long in happiness and contentment together.

Rereading the Text

For many readers, "Rapunzel" constructs very obvious gender roles through its plot and characters. But by challenging the dominant readings it is also possible to challenge cultural ideas about gender.

Here are two lists of characteristics commonly considered "masculine" and "feminine" in many cultures. In groups, develop arguments which explain how the qualities may be applied to the characters listed on the right.

"Masculine" Qualities	Characters
Active Mobile Public Rational Desiring	The husband The prince
"Feminine" Qualities	Characters
Passive Static Private Emotional Desirable	The wife Rapunzel

When you have completed the activity, try to repeat it with the pairings reversed. That is, develop arguments applying the masculine qualities to the two female characters and vice versa.

- How easy or difficult is it to do this reversal?
- Are some characters easier to reread than others? Which? Why?
- Can any of the characters be read as "transgressing" the gender categories above? (For example, the wife might be read as "desiring.") What effect does this have on possible readings of them?

The Witch

One character has been omitted from this activity—the witch. Discuss the following issues in your group:

- Which qualities from either group are most easily applied to the witch?
- Does this make her masculine or feminine, according to the lists?
- What does this suggest about how your particular culture views women who resist being slotted into the "feminine" mold? What might it suggest about the relationship between "women" and "power"?

Text and Culture

Modern theories suggest that reading practices involve "mapping" cultural knowledge onto textual features. This means that texts can be constructed in ways which make it easier or harder to impose the dominant reading. In the case of gender, texts which can be read more easily in dominant ways help the culture to "naturalize" gender. This enables patriarchal culture to pass off artificially constructed ideas as natural and therefore not in need of change.

Here is a list of possible beliefs and behaviors regarding gender. Which of them, in your view, can be "mapped" onto the text of "Rapunzel" most easily? Which, if any, does it seem to resist?

- Single women are objects of exchange between families.
- The exchange of women enables the family structure to reproduce itself.
- Single men have greater freedom than single women.
- Married men have less freedom than single men.
- Marriage confers increased status on couples.
- Power exercised by women rightly belongs to men.
- Women who have power are dangerous.
- Women who have power are not really women.

The Question of Masculinity

Most of the discussion to this point in the chapter has been concerned with representations of women. But concepts of masculinity are also culturally constructed. This is often concealed in patriarchal cultures. The dominant idea is that masculinity is "natural" and therefore not in need of analysis. The founder of psychoanalysis, Sigmund Freud, (1856–1939) had this to say:

> Throughout history people have knocked their heads against this riddle of femininity . . . . Nor will you have escaped worrying over this problem—those of you who are men; to those of you who are women this will not apply—you are yourselves the problem. (146)

The idea that femininity is a riddle, a "problem," is very strong in patriarchal culture. The effect of this is to deflect attention away from any study of masculinity, to hide it from view even though it is the dominant force.

"The Essence of a Man"

The next text we will consider has been described as a story

- about what it is to be a man;
- about the nature of manhood;
- about colonial oppression and exploitation;
- that explores the nature of masculinity;
- that both draws on and supports racist attitudes;
- that praises the universal virtues of loyalty and endurance;
- that excludes women as characters and as readers.

Before you read the story, discuss what might be meant by the title, "The Essence of a Man." Does "a Man" suggest a particular man or men in general? What is the essence of a man according to patriarchal culture? Contribute your ideas to a chalkboard list of features. Here are some starting points: courage, resourcefulness, strength . . .

Set in Canada, "The Essence of a Man" involves a sled journey across the snow between two camps. The character who makes the journey contends with blizzards, an attack by a lynx, and huskies which become savage and wild. While reading, check off items on your list as they seem to correspond with events in the story.

The Essence of a Man

Alan Sullivan

Through level lines of streaming snow, a huge figure loomed large and portentous. Vanishing in blinding gusts, it ever and ever appeared again, thrusting itself onward with dogged persistence. Across flat and frozen plains forged the great piston-like legs, driving down his snow-shoes with a clocklike regularity that suggested, rather than told of, enormous muscular force. Behind him, knee-deep, toiled five yellow-coated, black-muzzled dogs, their shoulders jammed tight into their collars, their tawny sides rippling with the play of straining tendons; and, last of all, a long, low toboggan lurched indomitably on, the trampled trail breaking into a surge of powdered snow under its curving bow.

Into the teeth of the gale pushed this pigmy caravan—a gale that was born on the flat shores of Hudson Bay, that breasted the slopes of the Height Land, that raged across the blank white expanse of Lac Seul, and was now shrieking down, dire and desolate, to the ice-bound and battlemented borders of Lake Superior. It was a wind that had weight. Tom Moore felt its vast and impalpable force, as he leaned against it, when he stopped for breath. It assaulted him—it tore steadily, relentlessly, at him, as if seeking to devour—it lashed the stinging grains into his face, and into the open mouths of his panting dogs—it smoothed out the crumpled trail as the wake of a ship is obliterated by closing waters—till, a moment after his passing, the snow ridges lay trackless and unruffled. Still, however insignificant in these formless wastes, that silent progress held steadfastly on; and so it had held from early morn. These black specs on a measureless counterpane, guided by some unfailing instinct that lurked far back in the big man's brain, were making an unswerving line for a wooded point that thrust out a faint and purple finger, far ahead in the gathering dusk. As they drew slowly in, the wind began to abate its force, and Tom, peering out from the mass of ice that was cemented to his mouth and eyes, looked for some sheltering haven. The dogs smelled the land, and more eagerly flung themselves into the taut traces, while over them gathered the shadows of the welcome woods.

Peter Anderson, the Hudson Bay factor at Lac Seul, was low in provisions, and had sent to the Ignace post a curt suggestion that the deficiency be supplied; and Tom Moore's laden toboggan was the brief but practical answer to his letter. The three-hundred-pound load was made up of the bare necessities of life—pork, flour, and the like; these, delivered, would be worth seventy-five cents a pound and thirty dollars a sack respectively; and Tom was the arbiter of transportation. In summer his canoe thrust its delicate bows through the waterways that interlaced the two posts, and in winter his snowshoes threaded the stark and frozen wilderness. He had always traveled alone on the ice. Nature had molded him with such a titan frame, so huge and powerful a body, so indomitable and fearless a soul that he had become accustomed to laughing at the fate that overtook many of his tribe. They disappeared every now and then, utterly, silently, and mysteriously; but ever Big Tom moved on, the incarnation of force and of life that mocked at death.

When, two days before, MacPherson had summoned him to the Ignace post, and pointed to the pile of provisions, and said laconically: "For Anderson, at Lac Seul," Tom had merely grunted, "How," and set out to harness his dogs. But the last day had brought him more serious reflection. By the flight of the goose it was two hundred miles and by the winter trail perhaps two hundred and fifteen; and of these forty now lay behind him.

He made his camp, he lit his fire, he flung to each ravenous dog a frozen whitefish, and ate, himself, almost as sparingly; then, rolled in his rabbit-skin blanket, he lay down on his back, and looked up at the winking stars.

At midnight the wind changed and veered into the south-east, bringing with it a clammy drizzle, half snow, half rain, that plastered the trees with a transparent enamel and spread over the surface of the earth a sheet of ice, half an inch thick, and exceeding sharp.

In that shivering hour which heralds the dawn, a branch cracked sharply a little distance from the camp. One of the dogs twitched an ear, and Tom was too deep in sleep to notice it. The five huskies were buried in snow beneath a tree, from a branch of which swung a sheaf of rigid fish, suspended in the air for security. But, in the half light, something moved, a something that turned upon the smouldering fire great luminous eyes—globes that seemed to receive the glow of dull coals, and give it out again in a changing iridescence. Around the eyes was a white mask, crowned by short, black-pointed ears; behind the ears moved noiselessly a tawny body, with heavy legs and broad, soft pads. It slipped from tree to tree, touching the ground lightly, here and there, till the great lynx hung, motionless and menacing, above the sleeping camp. It stopped, sniffed the tainted air, and then stared, fascinated, at the sheaf of fish, which hung, slowly revolving, in tantalizing proximity. Silently, with dainty and delicate caution, the lynx laid itself out on a branch, and, clinging tight, stretched out a curved forepaw; it just touched its object, and set it swaying. Again the paw went out, and again fell short. A quicker thrust, and the big pads slipped on the frozen wood, and, with a scream, the great cat fell fair on the sleeping dogs.

In an instant the air split with a frenzy of noise. Tom sprang up, saw a maelstrom of yellow forms, a convulsive, contorted mass, from which came the vicious snap of locking jaws, the yelp of agonized animals, and the short, coughing bark of the lynx. Around and in and out they rolled, buried in fur and snow. The wolf was born again in huskies, and, with all their primal ferocity, they assailed each other and a common enemy. Two of them crawled away, licking great wounds from deadly claws; and then gradually the battle waned, till it died in a fugue of howls, and the marauder escaped, torn and bleeding, into the silence from which he came.

Tom stood helpless, and then, when the three came limping home, went over to where his two best dogs lay, licking great gashes—for the lynx had literally torn them open. As he approached, they lifted their black lips till the long fangs shone, ivory white; and death and defiance gurgled in their throbbing throats. A glance told him that nothing could be done; the frost was already nipping the raw flesh till they snapped at their own vitals in desperation. He raised his axe, once, twice—and his two best huskies lay on a blanket of blood-stained snow, with twitching bodies and glazing eyes.

Then, very soberly, he examined the others. They were still fit for harness; so, in the yellow light that began to flood the world, he shortened his traces, twisted his feet in his toe straps, and, with never a look behind, faced again the burden of the day.

The trail was hard to break. The crust, that would not carry the dogs, was smashed down, and tilted cakes of ice fell over on his shoes, a deck load that made them a weariness to lift. Behind floundered the toiling huskies, the leader's nose glued to the tail of the trailing shoes. What vast reserve of strength did man and beast draw upon, Tom could not have told you; but, hour after hour, the small, indomitable train went on. As the day lengthened, Tom shortened his stride; for the dogs were evidently giving out, and his thigh muscles were burning like hot wires. At four o'clock the team stopped dead, the leader swaying in his tracks. The big man, running his hands over the shaking body, suddenly found one of them warm and wet—it was sticky with blood. Then he saw blood in the trail; looking back, he saw crimson spots as far as the eye could distinguish them; lifting the matted hide, he revealed a gash from which oozed great, slow drops. The valiant brute had drained his life out in a gory baptism of that killing trail. Then Tom sat down in dumb despair, took the lean yellow head upon his knees, smoothed the tawny fur back from those clouding eyes, and set his teeth hard as the dying beast licked his caressing hand in mute fidelity.

The great frame grew rigid as he watched, and slowly into the man's mind, for the first time in all his life, came doubt. Perhaps it was more wonderment. It was not any suggestion of failing powers, imminent danger, or impending hardships; it was rather a mute questioning of things which he had always heretofore accepted, as he did the rising and sinking sun—things which began and ended with the day. His reasonings were slow and laborious; his mind creaked, as it were, with effort—like an unused muscle, it responded with difficulty. Then, finally, he saw it all.

Long ago, when his mother died, she had warned him against the false new gods which the white man had brought from the big sea water, and in her old faith had turned her face to the wall of her tepee. She had been buried in a tree top, near a bend of the Albany River, where it turns north from Nepigon and runs through the spruce forests that slope down to Hudson's Bay. But Tom had listened to the new story—more than that, he had hewed square timber for the Mission Church at Ignace; and now—retribution had come at last. No sooner had the idea formulated itself, than it seized upon him; and then there rose to meet it—defiance. Grimly, he slackened the collar from the dead husky, and laid the empty traces across his own breast; savagely he thrust forward, and started the toboggan, and the diminishing company stayed and stopped not till, once again, the darkness came.

That night the two surviving dogs eyed him furtively, when he flung them their food. They did not devour it ravenously, as was their custom; but crouched, with the fish under their paws, and followed, with shifting look, every move he made. He was too weary to care; but, had he watched them an hour later, the sight would have convinced him that there was an evil spirit abroad in those frosty woods.

Noiselessly, they approached his sleeping form, sniffing intently at everything in the camp. He lay, massive and motionless, wrapped in an immense rabbit-skin blanket, one fold of which was thrown over the bag that held his provisions; his giant body was slack, relaxed, and full of great weariness.

The dogs moved without a sound, till they stood over the sleeping man. The long hair rose in ridges along their spines, as they put their noses to his robe, and sniffed at their unconscious master; for, whether it was the fight with the lynx, or that yellow body on the ice, some new and strange thing had come into their blood; they had reverted to the primal dog, and no longer felt the burden of the collar or trace—the labour of the trail had passed from them.

At first, the smell of man repelled them, but it was only for a moment; their lean shoulders swayed as their twitching noses ran over his outline, and then a new scent assailed them. It was the provision bag. Gently, and with infinite precaution, they pulled it. Tom stirred, but only stirred. The sack was trailed out over the snow, and the tough canvas soon gave way before those murderous teeth. In silence, and in hunger, they gorged; what they could not eat was destroyed, till, finally, with bulging sides, they lay down and slept, in utter repletion.

It was the sun on his face that woke Tom to a consciousness of what had happened. He felt for the bag, and, finding it not, looked for the dogs, and, on seeing them, raised his hand in anger. Now, this was a mistake; few dogs will wait for punishment, least of all a half-savage husky who expects it. He approached, they retreated; he stopped, they squatted on their haunches and eyed him suspiciously; he retreated, they did not move; he held out a fish, they were supremely indifferent. They had entered a new world, which was none of his; they suddenly found that they did not have to obey—and when man or beast reasons thus, it spells ruin. All his arts were exhausted and proved fruitless, and then Tom knew that an evil spirit—a Wendigo—was on his trail.

To push forward was his first instinct. Slowly, he rolled up the blanket, and laced it to the toboggan; and, as the sun topped the rim of the land, the unconquerable need struck out across the ice, the traces tugging at his shoulders. A few yards behind followed the enfranchised team, drunk with the intoxication of their new-found liberty. Never did he get within striking distance, but ever he was conscious of those soft, padding sounds; he felt as if they were always about to spring at his defenceless back, but all through the weary day they followed, elusive, mysteriously threatening.

He pulled up, faint with hunger, in mid-afternoon, and went into a thicket of cedar to set rabbit snares; but no sooner had he turned than the dogs were at the toboggan.

A ripping of canvas caught his ear, and he rushed back in fury. They fled at his approach, and lay, flat on the snow, their heads between their paws; so Tom pulled up his load, built a fire beside it, and watched the huskies till morning. He had now one hundred miles to go; he had three hundred pounds to pull, and no dogs; he could not, dare not sleep; and he had no food, but—Anderson was waiting at Lac Seul.

Who can enter into those next days? Through the storms—and they were many—moved a gigantic figure, and, after it, crawled a long coffin-like shape; and behind the shape trotted two wolfish forms, with lean flanks and ravenous jaws. Across the crystalline plains plodded the grim procession, and, at night, the red eye of a camp fire flung its flickering gleam on those same threatening forms, as they moved restlessly and noiselessly about, watching and waiting, waiting and watching. As his strength diminished with the miles, Tom began to see strange things and hear curious and pleasant sounds. Then he got very sleepy; the snow was just the color of the twenty-dollar blankets in the H.B. post; it was not cold now; he experienced a delicious langour; and people began to talk all around him; only they wouldn't answer when he shouted at them. Then the Wendigo came, and told him to lie down and rest, and, as he was taking off his shoes, another spirit called out: "Kago, kago—nebowah neepah panemah." ("Don't! Don't! You will find rest by and by.")

At noon, on the eighth day after Tom left Ignace post, Peter Anderson looked across the drifts of Lac Seul, and shook his head. The horizon was blotted out in a blizzard that whipped the flakes into his face like needle points, and the distance dissolved in a whirling view. The bush had been cleared away around his buildings, and, in the bare space, a mighty wind swooped and shrieked. As he turned, the gale lifted for a moment, and, infinitely remote, something appeared to break the snow line at the end of a long white lane of dancing wreaths; then the storm closed down, and the vision was lost. Keenly, he strained through half-closed lids; once more something stirred, and suddenly, the wind began to slacken. In the heart of it was staggering a giant shape, that swayed and tottered, but doggedly, almost unconsciously, moved on into the shelter of the land; behind trailed a formless mass, and, last of all, the apparition of two lank, limping dogs.

Drunkenly and unseeingly, but with blind, indomitable purpose, the man won every agonizing step. His snow-shoes were smashed to a shapeless tangle of wood and sinew; his face was gaunt, patched with grey blots of frost-bite; and, through his sunken cheeks, the high bones stood out like knuckles on a clenched fist. Ice was plastered on his cap, and lay fringed on brow and lids, but beneath them burned eyes that glowed with dull fires, quenchless and abysmal. By infinitesimal degrees he drew in, with not a wave of the hand, not a sign of recognition. Up the path, from shore to trading post, shouldered the titan figure, till it reached the door. At the latch, stiff, frozen fingers were fumbling as Anderson flung it open; and then a vast bulk darkened the threshold, swung in helpless hesitation for a fraction of time, and pitched, face foremost, on the rough pine floor.

A few hours later, he looked up from the pile of skins upon which Anderson had rolled him. His eyes wandered to the figure of the trader, who sat, serenely smoking, regarding with silent satisfaction a small mountain of provisions.

"All here, boss?"

"Ay, Tom, all here, and I'm mickle obliged to ye; are ye hungry Tom? Will ye hae a bit sup?"

"No eat for five days; pull toboggan. No dogs."

Anderson stiffened where he sat. "What's that? Haulin' three hunder' of grub, and ye were starving. Ye big copper-coloured fule!"

"No packer's grub, boss; Hudson Bay grub!"

It was almost a groan, for Tom was far spent.

Involuntarily the quiet Scot lifted his hands in amazement, and then hurried into his kitchen, murmuring, as he disappeared: "Man, man, it's with the likes of ye that the Hudson Bay keeps its word."

Reading against the Grain

Compare the items you have checked on the list of traditional features comprising the essence of a man; then discuss your reasons for checking each item.

Here is an alternative list of qualities which might comprise "the essence of a man." In a patriarchal culture, many of these terms will have negative connotations when applied to men.

fearfulness	stubbornness	fragility	sentimentality
subordination	powerlessness	compassion	stupidity
dependence	foolishness	irrationality	cruelty

Working in groups, develop statements which "reread" the characters in terms of this second list. Use the following structure for your statements:

■ Tom is fearful when . . .
■ Anderson is cruel when . . .

Are there any statements which you cannot complete? How does this rereading alter your response to the title, "The Essence of a Man"?

Deconstructing the Text

The title of the story, by relying on cultural myths about masculinity, invites an "innocent" reading which focuses on the concept of "manliness." But the text supports many other readings, which are not at all innocent.

It supports, for example, unacceptable values about the exploitation of indigenous races by colonizing races. Tom is being used by Anderson and McPherson to do hard and dangerous work, but the story chooses to ignore the unequal power relationship. Instead, it invites praise for Tom's loyalty—an insulting suggestion, if you think about it.

This story, it can be argued, is told in the interests of a particular group of people: white, middle-class, colonizing males.

In Pairs

Collect fragments of writing which could be used to support:

- ▪ a "dehumanized" reading of Tom by giving him the attributes of a machine or tool, e.g., "piston-like legs" or "making an unswerving line";
- ▪ the idea that McPherson and Anderson are "civilized," the brains of the operation, e.g., "serenely smoking" or "McPherson had summoned him."

Writing

Drawing on the work you have done in this chapter, explore in writing your reasons for agreeing or disagreeing with this description of the story:

> "This story explores universal themes of endurance and achievement in the face of hardship. It reveals the true nature of the human spirit: a combination of individual courage, comradeship, and dedication that is the basis of civilization."

New Perspectives: "Nice Men"

In addition to rereading texts from the position of groups that are often marginalized or silenced in dominant readings, increasing numbers of women are writing with the aim of constructing a feminine perspective.

Nice Men

Dorothy Byrne

I know a nice man who is kind to his wife
and always lets her do what she wants.

I heard of another nice man who killed his
girlfriend. It was an accident. He pushed her
in a quarrel and she split her skull on the
dining-room table. He was such a guilt-ridden
sight in court that the jury felt sorry for him.

Me friend Aiden is nice. He thinks women are
really equal.

There are lots of nice men who help their wives
with the shopping and the housework.

And many men, when you are alone with them, say, "I prefer women. They are so understanding." This is another example of men being nice.

Some men, when you make a mistake at work, just laugh. They don't go on about it or shout. That's nice.

At times, the most surprising men will say at parties, "There's a lot to this Women's Lib." Here again, is a case of men behaving in a nice way.

Another nice thing is that some men are sympathetic when their wives feel unhappy. I've often heard men say, "Don't worry about everything so much, dear."

You hear stories of men who are far more than nice—putting women in lifeboats first, etc.

Sometimes when a man has not been nice, he apologizes and trusts you with intimate details of the pressures in his life. This just shows how nice he is, underneath.

I think that is all I can say on the subject of nice men. Thank you.

Working in pairs, practice reading "Nice Men" aloud. Is it possible to vary the tone of your reading in such a way as to construct different "readings"? Try to develop ways of presenting the poem orally in a manner which suggests the speaker is (a) innocent and sincere; (b) sarcastic; (c) angry.

Whose Reading?

It will be apparent already that "Nice Men" can be read in a number of ways. Here are two possibilities:

■ as a sincere, innocent statement about some of the ways in which men are kind to women;

■ as an ironic or sarcastic statement about how superficial and trivial men's attitudes toward women are.

1. How does the meaning of "nice" differ in these two readings of the poem?

2. Discuss some of the examples of "niceness" listed in the poem. For each, explain (a) why some people would consider this action or attitude genuinely nice, and (b) why some people might find it patronizing or offensive.

3. On what basis is it possible to choose between these two readings? Can one be proved to be a more accurate reading than the other?

4. Which groups of people might support each of the two readings? Why? Whose interests might be served by each reading?

Revisions: "The Company of Wolves"

Another of the ways in which some feminist writers are challenging the traditional or dominant readings of gender in literary texts is by retelling or rewriting some of their cultures' stories. This retelling or rewriting is sometimes called "re-vision," implying that the work is both revised and shaped by a new vision—a feminist vision.

Angela Carter (1940–) is a feminist writer who has retold many popular fairy tales. Some of her stories have been made into successful films, as is the case with "The Company of Wolves."

As a Class

"The Company of Wolves" can be read as a re-vision of "Little Red Riding Hood," a story which many feminist readings find objectionable.

1. From memory, reconstruct the characters and events of "Little Red Riding Hood," and create a chalkboard summary of the story.

2. The story of Red Riding Hood can be offered as a lesson to young girls. When used in this way, it supports beliefs such as the following.

   ◾ Girls should never stray from the path or something terrible may happen to them.
   ◾ If misfortune befalls a young girl, it is her own fault; she cannot expect the "wolves" to change their behavior.
   ◾ If a young girl is in trouble, her only hope is that a gentleman will come to her rescue.

   What other lessons does this reading of the story provide?

3. Why doesn't the story question the behavior of the wolves? Is it a case of "boys will be boys," so girls have to take care? What other gender-related issues are raised by the story?

"The Company of Wolves"

In this story, Angela Carter draws on some traditional ideas about men and wolves, but she adds some modern twists. Read the story, and then work through the activities which follow it.

The Company of Wolves

Angela Carter

One beast and only one howls in the woods by night.

The wolf is carnivore incarnate and he's as cunning as he is ferocious; once he's had a taste of flesh then nothing else will do.

At night, the eyes of wolves shine like candle flames, yellowish, reddish, but that is because the pupils of their eyes fatten on darkness and catch the light from your lantern to flash it back to you—red for danger; if a wolf's eyes reflect only moonlight, then they gleam a cold and unnatural green, a mineral, a piercing colour. If the benighted traveller spies those luminous, terrible sequins stitched suddenly on the black thickets, then he knows he must run, if fear has not struck him stock-still.

But those eyes are all you will be able to glimpse of the forest assassins as they cluster invisibly around your smell of meat as you go through the wood unwisely late. They will be like shadows, they will be like wraiths, grey members of a congregation of nightmare; hark! his long, wavering howl . . . an aria of fear made audible.

The wolfsong is the sound of the rending you will suffer, in itself a murdering.

It is winter and cold weather. In this region of mountain and forest, there is now nothing for the wolves to eat. Goats and sheep are locked up in the byre, the deer departed for the remaining pasturage on the southern slopes—wolves grow lean and famished. There is so little flesh on them that you could count the starveling ribs through their pelts, if they gave you time before they pounced. Those slavering jaws; the lolling tongue; the rime of saliva on the grizzled chops—of all the teeming perils of the night and the forest, ghosts, hobgoblins, ogres that grill babies upon gridirons, witches that fatten their captives in cages for cannibal tables, the wolf is worst for he cannot listen to reason.

You are always in danger in the forest, where no people are. Step between the portals of the great pines where the shaggy branches tangle about you, trapping the unwary traveller in nets as if the vegetation itself were in a plot with the wolves who live there, as though the wicked trees go fishing on behalf of their friends—step between the gateposts of the forest with the greatest trepidation and infinite precautions, for if you stray from the path for one instant, the wolves will eat you. They are grey as famine, they are as unkind as plague.

The grave-eyed children of the sparse villages always carry knives with them when they go out to tend the little flocks of goats that provide the homesteads with acrid milk and rank, maggoty cheeses. Their knives are half as big as they are, the blades are sharpened daily.

But the wolves have ways of arriving at your own hearthside. We try and try but sometimes we cannot keep them out. There is no winter's night the cottager does not fear to see a lean, grey, famished snout questing under the door, and there was a woman once bitten in her own kitchen as she was straining the macaroni.

Fear and flee the wolf; for, worst of all, the wolf may be more than he seems. There was a hunter once, near here, that trapped a wolf in a pit. This wolf had massacred the sheep and goats; eaten up a mad old man who used to live by himself in a hut halfway up the mountain and sing to Jesus all day; pounced on a girl looking after the sheep, but she made such a commotion that men came with rifles and scared him away and tried to track him in the forest but he was cunning and easily gave them the slip. So this hunter dug a pit and put a duck in it, for bait, all alive-oh; and he covered the pit with straw smeared with wolf dung. Quack, quack! went the duck and a wolf came slinking out of the forest, a big one, a heavy one, he weighed as much as a grown man and the straw gave way beneath him—into the pit he tumbled. The hunter jumped down after him, slit his throat, cut off all his paws for a trophy.

And then no wolf at all lay in front of the hunter but the bloody trunk of a man, headless, footless, dying, dead.

A witch from up the valley once turned an entire wedding party into wolves because the groom had settled on another girl. She used to order them to visit her, at night, from spite, and they would sit and howl around her cottage for her, serenading her with their misery.

Not so very long ago, a young woman in our village married a man who vanished clean away on her wedding night. The bed was made with new sheets and the bride lay down in it; the groom said he was going out to relieve himself, insisted on it, for the sake of decency, and she drew the coverlet up to her chin and she lay there. And she waited and she waited and then she waited again—surely he's been gone a long time? Until she jumps up in bed and shrieks to hear a howling, coming on the wind of the forest.

That long-drawn, wavering howl has, for all its fearful resonance, some inherent sadness in it, as if the beasts would love to be less beastly if only they knew how and never cease to mourn their own condition. There is a vast melancholy in the canticles of the wolves, melancholy infinite as the forest, endless as these long nights of winter and yet that ghastly sadness, that mourning for their own, irreme-diable appetites, can never move the heart for not one phrase in it hints at the possibility of redemption; grace could not come to the wolf from its own despair, only through some external mediator, so that, sometimes, the beast will look as if he half welcomes the knife that despatches him.

The young woman's brothers searched the outhouses and the haystacks but never found any remains so the sensible girl dried her eyes and found herself another husband not too shy to piss into a pot who spent nights indoors. She gave him a pair of bonny babies and all went right as a trivet until, one freezing night, the night of the solstice, the hinge of the year when things do not fit together as well as they should, the longest night, her first good man came home again.

A great thump on the door announced him as she was stirring the soup for the father of her children and she knew him the moment she lifted the latch to him although it was years since she'd worn black for him and now he was in rags and his hair hung down his back and never saw a comb, alive with lice.

"Here I am again, missus," he said. "Get me my bowl of cabbage and be quick about it."

Then her second husband came in with wood for the fire and when the first one saw she'd slept with another man and, worse, clapped his red eyes on her little children who'd crept into the kitchen to see what all the din was about, he shouted: "I wish I were a wolf again, to teach this whore a lesson!" So a wolf he instantly became and tore off the eldest boy's left foot before he was chopped up with the hatchet they used for chopping logs. But when the wolf lay bleeding and gasping its last, the pelt peeled off again and he was just as he had been, years ago, when he ran away from his marriage bed, so that she wept and her second husband beat her.

They say there's an ointment the Devil gives you that turns you into a wolf the minute you rub it on. Or, that he was born feet first and had a wolf for his father and his torso is a man's but his legs and genitals are a wolf's. And he has a wolf's heart.

Seven years is a werewolf's natural span but if you burn his human clothing you condemn him to wolfishness for the rest of his life, so old wives hereabouts think it some protection to throw a hat or an apron at the werewolf, as if clothes made the man. Yet by the eyes, those phosphorescent eyes, you know him in all his shapes; the eyes alone unchanged by metamorphosis.

Before he can become a wolf, the lycanthrope strips stark naked. If you spy a naked young man among the pines, you must run as if the Devil were after you.

It is midwinter and the robin, the friend of man, sits on the handle of the gardener's spade and sings. It is the worst time in all the year for wolves but this strong-minded child insists she will go off through the wood. She is quite sure the wild beasts cannot harm her although, well-warned, she lays a carving knife in the basket her mother has packed with cheeses. There is a bottle of harsh liquor distilled from brambles; a batch of flat oatcakes baked on the hearthstone; a pot or two of jam. The flaxen-haired girl will take these delicious gifts to a reclusive grandmother so old the burden of her years is crushing her to death. Granny lives two hours' trudge through the winter woods; the child wraps herself up in her thick shawl, draws it over her head. She steps into her stout wooden shoes; she is dressed and ready and it is Christmas Eve. The malign door of the solstice still swings upon its hinges but she has been too much loved ever to feel scared.

Children do not stay young for long in this savage country. There are no toys for them to play with so they work hard and grow wise but this one, so pretty and the youngest of her family, a little late-comer, had been indulged by her mother and the grandmother who'd knitted her the red shawl that, today, has the ominous if brilliant look of blood on snow. Her breasts have just begun to swell; her hair is like lint, so fair it hardly makes a shadow on her pale forehead; her cheeks are an emblematic scarlet and white and she has just started her woman's bleeding, the clock inside her that will strike, henceforward, once a month.

She stands and moves within the invisible pentacle of her own virginity. She is an unbroken egg; she is a sealed vessel; she has inside her a magic space the entrance to which is shut tight with a plug of membrane; she is a closed system; she does not know how to shiver. She has her knife and she is afraid of nothing.

Her father might forbid her, if he were home, but he is away in the forest, gathering wood, and her mother cannot deny her.

The forest closed upon her like a pair of jaws.

There is always something to look at in the forest, even in the middle of winter—the huddled mounds of birds, succumbed to the lethargy of the season, heaped on the creaking boughs and too forlorn to sing; the bright frills of the winter fungi on the blotched trunks of the trees; the cuneiform slots of rabbits and deer, the herringbone tracks of the birds, a hare as lean as a rasher of bacon streaking across the path where the thin sunlight dapples the russet brakes of last year's bracken.

When she heard the freezing howl of a distant wolf, her practiced hand sprang to the handle of her knife, but she saw no sign of a wolf at all, nor a naked man, neither, but then she heard a clattering among the brushwood and there sprang on to the path a fully clothed one, a very handsome young one, in the green coat and wideawake hat of a hunter, laden with carcasses of game birds. She had her hand on her knife at the first rustle of twigs but he laughed with a flash of white teeth when he saw her and made her a comic yet flattering little bow; she'd never seen such a fine fellow before, not among the rustic clowns of her native village. So on they went together, through the thickening light of the afternoon.

Soon they were laughing and joking like old friends. When he offered to carry her basket, she gave it to him although her knife was in it because he told her his rifle would protect them. As the day darkened, it began to snow again; she felt the first flakes settle on her eyelashes but now there was only half a mile to go and there would be a fire, and hot tea, and a welcome, a warm one, surely, for the dashing huntsman as well as herself.

This young man had a remarkable object in his pocket. It was a compass. She looked at the little round glass face in the palm of his hand and watched the wavering needle with a vague wonder. He assured her this compass had taken him safely through the wood on his hunting trip because the needle always told him with perfect accuracy where the north was. She did not believe it; she knew she should never leave the path on the way through the wood or else she would be lost instantly. He laughed at her again; gleaming trails of spittle clung to his teeth. He said, if he plunged off the path into the forest that surrounded them, he could guarantee to arrive at her grandmother's house a good quarter of an hour before she did, plotting his way through the undergrowth with his compass, while she trudged the long way, along the winding path.

I don't believe you. Besides, aren't you afraid of the wolves?

He only tapped the gleaming butt of his rifle and grinned.

Is it a bet? he asked her. Shall we make a game of it? What will you give me if I get to your grandmother's house before you?

What would you like? she asked disingenuously.

A kiss.

Commonplaces of a rustic seduction; she lowered her eyes and blushed.

He went through the undergrowth and took her basket with him but she forgot to be afraid of the beasts, although now the moon was rising, for she wanted to dawdle on her way to make sure the handsome gentleman would win his wager.

Grandmother's house stood by itself a little way out of the village. The freshly falling snow blew in eddies about the kitchen garden and the young man stepped delicately up the snowy path to the door as if he were reluctant to get his feet wet, swinging his bundle of game and the girl's basket and humming a little tune to himself.

There is a faint trace of blood on his chin; he has been snacking on his catch.

He rapped on the panels with his knuckles.

Aged and frail, granny is three-quarters succumbed to the mortality the ache in her bones promises her and almost ready to give in entirely. A boy came out from the village to build her hearth for the night an hour ago and the kitchen crackles with busy firelight. She has her Bible for company, she is a pious old woman. She is propped up on several pillows in the bed set into the wall peasant-fashion, wrapped up in the patchwork quilt she made before she was married, more years ago than she cares to remember. Two china spaniels with liver-coloured blotches on their coats and black noses sit on either side of the fireplace. There is a bright rug of woven rags on the pantiles. The grandfather clock ticks away her eroding time.

We keep wolves outside by living well.

He rapped upon the panels with his hairy knuckles.

It is your granddaughter, he mimicked in a high soprano.

Lift up the latch and walk in, my darling.

You can tell them by their eyes, eyes of a beast of prey, nocturnal, devastating eyes as red as a wound; you can hurl your Bible at him and your apron after, granny, you thought that was sure prophylactic against these infernal vermin . . . now call on Christ and his mother and all the angels in heaven to protect you but it won't do you any good.

His feral muzzle is sharp as a knife; he drops his golden burden of gnawed pheasant on the table and puts down the dear girl's basket, too. Oh, my God, what have you done with her?

Off with his disguise, that coat of forest coloured cloth, the hat with feather tucked into the ribbon; his matted hair streams down his white shirt and she can see the lice moving in it. The sticks in the hearth shift and hiss; night and the forest has come into the kitchen with darkness tangled in its hair.

He strips off his shirt. His skin is the colour and texture of vellum. A crisp stripe of hair runs down his belly, his nipples are ripe and dark as poison fruit but he's so thin you could count the ribs under his skin if only he gave you the time. He strips off his trousers and she can see how hairy his legs are. His genitals huge. Ah! huge.

The last thing the old lady saw in all this world was a young man, eyes like cinders, naked as a stone, approaching her bed.

The wolf is carnivore incarnate.

When he had finished with her, he licked his chops and quickly dressed himself again, until he was just as he had been when he came through the door. He burned the inedible hair in the fireplace and wrapped the bones up in a napkin that he hid away under the bed in the wooden chest in which he found a clean pair of sheets. These he carefully put on the bed instead of the tell-tale stained ones he stowed away in the laundry basket. He plumped up the pillows and shook out the patch-work quilt, he picked up the Bible from the floor, closed it and laid it on the table. All was as it had been before except that grandmother was gone. The sticks twitched in the grate, the clock ticked and the young man sat patiently, deceitfully beside the bed in granny's nightcap.

Rat-a-tap-tap.

Who's there, he quavers in granny's antique falsetto.

Only your granddaughter.

So she came in, bringing with her a flurry of snow that melted in tears on the tiles, and perhaps she was a little disappointed to see only her grandmother sitting beside the fire. But then he flung off the blanket and sprang to the door, pressing his back against it so that she could not get out again.

The girl looked around the room and saw there was not even the indentation of a head on the smooth cheek of the pillow and how, for the first time she'd seen it so, the Bible lay closed on the table. The tick of the clock cracked like a whip. She wanted her knife from her basket but she did not dare reach for it because his eyes were fixed upon her—huge eyes that now seemed to shine with a unique, interior light, eyes the size of saucers, saucers full of Greek fire, diabolic phosphorescence.

What big eyes you have.

All the better to see you with.

No trace at all of the old woman except for a tuft of white hair that had caught in the bark of an unburned log. When the girl saw that, she knew she was in danger of death.

Where is my grandmother?

There's nobody here but we two, my darling.

Now a great howling rose up all around them, near, very near, as close as the kitchen garden, the howling of a multitude of wolves; she knew the worst wolves are hairy on the inside and she shivered, in spite of the scarlet shawl she pulled more closely round herself as if it could protect her although it was as red as the blood she must spill.

Who has come to sing us carols, she said.

Those are the voices of my brothers, darling; I love the company of wolves. Look out of the window and you'll see them.

Snow half-caked the lattice and she opened it to look into the garden. It was a white night of moon and snow; the blizzard whirled round the gaunt, grey beasts who squatted on their haunches among the rows of winter cabbages, pointing their sharp snouts to the moon and howling as if their hearts would break. Ten wolves; twenty wolves—so many wolves she could not count them, howling in concert as if demented or deranged. Their eyes reflected the light from the kitchen and shone like a hundred candles.

It is very cold, poor things, she said; no wonder they howl so.

She closed the window on the wolves' threnody and took off her scarlet shawl, the colour of poppies, the colour of sacrifices, the colour of her menses, and, since her fear did her no good, she ceased to be afraid.

What shall I do with my shawl?

Throw it on the fire, dear one. You won't need it again.

She bundled up her shawl and threw it on the blaze, which instantly consumed it. Then she drew her blouse over her head; her small breasts gleamed as if the snow had invaded the room.

What shall I do with my blouse?

Into the fire with it, too, my pet.

The thin muslin went flaring up the chimney like a magic bird and now off came her skirt, her woollen stockings, her shoes, and on to the fire they went, too, and were gone for good. The firelight shone through the edges of her skin; now she was clothed only in her untouched integument of flesh. Thus dazzling, naked she combed out her hair with her fingers; her hair looked white as the snow outside. Then went directly to the man with red eyes in whose unkempt mane the lice moved; she stood up on tiptoe and unbuttoned the collar of his shirt.

What big arms you have.

All the better to hug you with.

Every wolf in the world now howled a prothalamion outside the window as she freely gave him the kiss she owed him.

What big teeth you have!

She saw how his jaw began to slaver and the room was full of the clamour of the forest's Liebestod but the wise child never flinched, even when he answered:

All the better to eat you with.

The girl burst out laughing; she knew she was nobody's meat. She laughed at him full in the face, she ripped off his shirt for him and flung it into the fire, in the fiery wake of her own discarded clothing. The flames danced like dead souls on Walpurgisnacht and the old bones under the bed set up a terrible clattering but she did not pay them any heed.

Carnivore incarnate, only immaculate flesh appeases him.

She will lay his fearful head upon her lap and she will pick out the lice into her mouth and eat them, as he will bid her, as she would do in a savage marriage ceremony.

The blizzard will die down.

The blizzard died down, leaving the mountains as randomly covered with snow as if a blind woman had thrown a sheet over them, the upper branches of the forest pines limed, creaking, swollen with the fall.

Snowlight, moonlight, a confusion of paw-prints.

All silent, all still.

Midnight; and the clock strikes. It is Christmas Day, the werewolves' birthday, the door of the solstice stands wide open; let them all sink through.

See! sweet and sound she sleeps in granny's bed, between the paws of the tender wolf.

On Your Own

Write about your reactions to the story in journal form. That is, record your thoughts and impressions about it, in any order and any form you like. These notes are for your own use, to help you sort out your thoughts. When you have finished writing, discuss your reaction with other members of your group.

In Groups

Here is one reading of the fairy tale "Little Red Riding Hood." It may suggest why many feminist readings challenge the story.

> The story is really a "cautionary tale." It warns young girls of the dangers which await them in the big, wide world—dangers from creatures which lurk in the dark, away from "the path." It teaches us that good little girls do exactly as they are told and stay on the right track, a path which links mother, grandmother, and daughter in fear and obedience. It teaches us that women had better stay inside if they know what's good for them, and that they have no one to blame if they allow themselves to be led "astray." Wolves, on the other hand, rule the world outside the home. It is in their nature to be cunning, and to prey on little girls. They are not to be blamed for this; it is just the way things are. The only things which can keep a girl safe from them are her own common sense and a man who is handy with an axe.

1. How does this reading of the story serve the interests of a patriarchal society? How does it serve to keep women "in their place"?

2. Is it possible to read Angela Carter's story in this way? If not, what aspects of the story challenge or disrupt such a reading?

3. How is femininity constructed in Carter's story? Make a list of all the qualities which the young girl in the story seems to represent. How do they differ from the qualities represented by Red Riding Hood in the fairy tale?

Writing

1. Using the paragraph above as an example, produce a brief reading of Angela Carter's story. Whose interests are served by Carter's story? Does it serve patriarchy, for instance, or does it suggest that women need not be meek and afraid?

2. Select a fairy tale which constructs either traditional or unusual gender roles for its characters and readers. Explain how you think gender is constructed in the text, and discuss the role played by such stories in your culture.

3. Write your own "re-vision" of a popular fairy tale. Can you produce a story which resists the dominant reading which appears to be invited by the fairy tale?

References

Austen, Jane. "Emma and Edgar: A Tale." *Minor Works*. Ed. R. W. Chapman. London: Oxford UP, 1954.

Ayres, Pam. "Good-Bye Worn Out Morris 1000." *All Pam's Poems*. London: Hutchinson, 1978.

Byrne, Dorothy. "Nice Men." *Is That the New Moon?* Ed. Wendy Cope. London: William Collins, 1989.

Carter, Angela. "The Company of Wolves." *The Bloody Chamber*. London: Victor Gollancz, 1979.

Chmelnitzky, Alix. "Rest in Peace." *The Anduril*. Ed. F. Courtney and K. Marais de la Motte. Mosman Park, Austral.: St. Hilda's ASG Publications, 1998.

Cowan, Peter. "School." *The Unploughed Land*. North Ryde, New South Wales: Collins/Angus and Robertson, 1958.

Creely, Robert. "I Know a Man." *Mainly Modern*. Ed. John Colmer. Adelaide: Rigby Heinemann, 1969.

Dickens, Charles. *Hard Times*. London: Heinemann Educational, 1960.

Donne, John. "A Valediction: Forbidding Mourning." *Poems: Wadsworth Handbook and Anthology*. Ed. Charles Frederick Main and Peter J. Seng. San Francisco: Wadsworth, 1961.

Fowles, John. *The Collector*. New York: Little, 1998.

Frame, Janet. "A Night of Frost and a Morning of Mist." *Snowman, Snowman: Fables and Fantasies*. New York: G. Braziller, 1963.

Freud, Sigmund. *New Introductory Lectures on Psychoanalysis*. Trans. James Strachey. Vol. 2. London: Penguin, 1973.

Frost, Robert. "The Aim Was Song." *Selected Poems of Robert Frost*. New York: Holt, 1963.

———. "Never Again Would Birds' Song Be the Same." *Selected Poems of Robert Frost*. New York: Holt, 1963.

Johnson, Eva. "Weevilly Porridge." *Inside Black Australia*. Ed. Kevin Gilbert. Ringwood, Victoria: Penguin, 1988.

Johnson, Linton Kwesi. "Yout Scene." *Dread, Beat 'n Blood*. London: Bogle-L'Ouverture, 1975.

Moffitt, Ian. "Leisure." *This is Australia*. Ed. Rudolph Brasch. Sydney: Paul Hamlyn, 1979.

Nichols, Grace. "Beauty." *The Fat Black Woman's Poems*. London: Virago, 1984.

Richards, I. A. *Practical Criticism: A Study of Literary Judgment*. New York: Harcourt, 1963.

Roueche, Berton. "Phone Call." *New Yorker*. 25 Aug. 1965.

"Rapunzel." *Grimm's Fairy Tales*. Trans. Vladimir Varecha. London: Cathay, 1979.

Sullivan, Alan. "The Essence of a Man." *Oul-I-But and Other Stories*. London: J. M. Dent, 1913.

Tennyson, Alfred. "The Eagle." *Poems: Wadsworth Handbook and Anthology.* Ed. Charles Frederick Main and Peter J. Seng. San Francisco: Wadsworth, 1961.

Wordsworth, William. "To a Butterfly." *Selected Poems and Prefaces.* Ed. Jack Stillinger. Boston: Houghton, 1965.